Y0-ABF-605

The Joy of Birding

The Joy of Birding

A GUIDE TO BETTER BIRDWATCHING

CHUCK BERNSTEIN

Introduction by Roger Tory Peterson

Capra Press
1984

Copyright ©1984 by Charles Bernstein.
All rights reserved. Printed in the U.S.A.

Editing by Judith Young
Editorial Assistance by Terri Wright Macrae
Illustration by Karen Foster and Daniel Randolph.
Typography and design by Jim Cook/Santa Barbara.

LIBRARY OF CONGRESS CATALOGING IN PUBLICATION DATA
Bernstein, Charles, 1919-
   The joy of birding.
   Includes index.
   1. Birdwatching.   I. Title.
Z1677.5.B44   1984   598'.07'234   84-7778
ISBN 0-88496-220-2 (pbk.)

Published by CAPRA PRESS
Post Office Box 2068
Santa Barbara, California 93120

Contents.

6

The Joy of Birding

Acknowledgements.

For my material, boundless in scope, I feel I should thank every birdwatcher who has gone before me. Albeit unknowingly, each has in some way contributed a feather—perhaps merely a barbule—to the "feathering out" of these birding tales and birding tips. I thank Bill and Elsa Thompson, publishers, and particularly Mary Bowers and Pat Murphy, editors of *Bird Watcher's Digest,* for publishing my stories and essays, where many of these chapters (since updated, revised and "sanitized") first saw the light of day in my "Birding Tips" column. I thank the Los Angeles County Museum of Natural History, Section of Ornithology, its curator, Dr. Ralph Schreiber, and especially Kimball Garrett, its collections manager, for the many kindnesses and use of the bird-study skin collections; Dr. H. Lee Jones and Paul Lehman for helpful suggestions and advice.

But for the many long discussions, the exchange of ideas, and the many days together in the field during which he pointed out so much about the birds, I especially thank Jon Dunn, a California birder of world class whom I led on some of his earliest birdwalks. A classic case of teacher becoming student.

Introduction.

It was on the shores of Salton Sea, near the Mexican border with California, that I first met Chuck Bernstein, although I had previously enjoyed his essays in the *Bird Watcher's Digest*. The bird that brought us like a magnet to this broad expanse of saline water in the desert was a Spotted Redshank in full breeding plumage, a sandpiper thousands of miles from its home in Asia. We were joined by scores of other binocular addicts who had been alerted to this *rara avis* by the birders' hot-line.

Not everyone is turned on by birding, but hundreds of thousands are; it is one of the fastest-growing sports in our country. To Chuck Bernstein it has become a passion from which he has never freed himself. In this very readable book he recounts some of his adventures and tells us what makes a birder tick.

For me, birds have been an obsession ever since I was eleven years old in the seventh grade in Jamestown, New York. Our teacher, Miss Blanche Hornbeck, a young red-headed lady in her early thirties, formed a Junior Audubon Club. We colored the outline drawings that accompanied the junior leaflets and Miss Hornbeck gave each of us a Fuertes colorplate from the portfolio of *The Birds of New York State* to copy. Mine was the Blue Jay.

I have often wondered why, in a classroom of twenty-five or thirty, I was the only one who became hooked on birds for life. Reflecting on this, I suspect that I was turned on by an event that happened on my very first field trip. I can even recall the exact date and time—April 8, 1920, in the early morning—when a pal and I crossed the railroad tracks and climbed Swede Hill to explore new terrain.

13

As we entered a grove of maples beyond the edge of town I spotted a bundle of brown feathers clinging to the trunk of a tree. It was a flicker, its head buried in the fluffed-up feathers of its back. It was asleep, probably exhausted from migration, but I thought it was dead. Gingerly I touched it and instantaneously it exploded into life, jerked its head free of its feathers, revealing the scarlet nape patch, and then with a flash of golden wings, dashed away among the trees. What had seemed like an inert, dead thing was very much alive. It was like resurrection—an affirmation of life. Ever since, birds have seemed to me to be the most vivid expression of the natural world, which to many of us is the "real" world.

The observation of birds can be many things—an art, a science, a tradition, or a recreation. It can also be a sport, ticking them off on a scorecard—"ornithogolfing" if you will—and like all games it can be very competitive. The hundreds of thousands who enjoy the fun and games of this hobby prefer to call themselves birders rather than birdwatchers. To them "the list is the thing." Birdwatcher is a more inclusive term which might include *anyone* who looks at birds, from the chickadee type of birdwatcher who simply feeds birds at the kitchen window all the way to the academic who belongs to the American Ornithologists Union.

Birding has become far more sophisticated than it was when I wrote and illustrated my first *Field Guide to the Birds*, fifty years ago. We were just emerging from the era of bird identification by shotgun, and the concept of "field marks" was relatively new. Some of today's superstars no longer rely on mere binoculars and spotting scopes; they now use Celestrons and Questars, instruments intended for the amateur astronomer and which cost astronomical prices. With a Questar you can see even the nasal grooves on a Polynesian Tattler. Birding on that level has come almost full cycle back to the specimen tray, which prompts some to ask, Is it as much fun?

I think so; the birds are still *alive*.

ROGER TORY PETERSON

Foreword.

I write about birding because I have to. I am that eager to pass on birding tips which can make birdwatching easier, more accurate and more enjoyable. It is both comical and pathetic to look back on the haphazard course of my own early years in the sport. I learned little then; there were too few around who cared to teach. As do most beginners, I flipped through the field guides, playing the matchup game with every bird I saw, while in my own mind I was never quite content that this was the bird and never quite certain there wasn't a picture on still another page that it might be.

Long ago I realized that many of the time-proven birding tips I received from old-timers were being passed on from generation to generation orally, they had never been put into print, and with time much of it would be lost forever. I became aware, too, that recent discoveries about the world of birds, including marks that can identify species, are published in scientific and semi-scientific journals and are disguised in the arcane jargon of the professional ornithologists.

This volume is my unabashed attempt to expand the horizons of birdwatchers beyond mere species identification and the admittedly great sport of listing into the study of birds as living animals. Learning about distribution, migration, molt and plumage changes, feeding habits and other details will give you a much deeper understanding of the natural world. The more knowledge you have, the more accurate your field notes and the more careful your identifications.

For me every birdwalk is an adventure, imbued with romance. From where and how far has each bird come? Where is it going? How

15

do resident birds survive the year-round in your location? No matter how parochial the area or how commonplace the birds, there is always some new excitement, always something to be learned by watching carefully. Come walk beside me—beginner, enthusiast, expert—and share some of my birding trips.

NOTE

At the end of some chapters are lists of specific birds sighted by Mr. Bernstein on the birding trips described in that chapter. The birds are in the same order they were spotted, and the lists include both common and Latin names. See the table of contents for specific page numbers.

1.
Leave Those Field Guides at Home: Birding British Style.

How CAN you become a better birder? What is the key to birding know-how, especially bird identification? Which method is the most efficient and meaningful? There are as many answers to these questions as there are birding experts, and here in North America we have fortunately been blessed with many such experts. In the last half-century, creative, talented people have produced fine illustrations and paintings and have written excellent field guides, dramatically increasing an informed birdwatching public.

The appearance of our first field guides was the greatest thing that could have happened to birding, of course. It immediately wiped away the stigma associated with watching birds; and by simplifying identification and opening up the subject to the broad general public, birding was elevated to what is probably the fastest-growing sport in America. The truth is, the guide writers created birdwatching as the great hobby it has become—as, indeed, the subculture it has become, with its own jargon, its own literature and, for some, its own way of life. And the birding community owes these pioneers everlasting respect and gratitude.

The way to learn the birds was to carry a bird book or two into the field and match up a picture with a bird. This system was indeed encouraged by the sale of the books—and even of pouches to carry them in—at meetings of most birdwatching groups, and especially at meetings of the Audubon Society throughout the country. One still finds even advanced birders carrying the books into the field with them.

But one is aware now of an ever-growing feeling that this is an improper use of field guides, one that does not contribute very much to the learning process; a feeling that there is an overuse, a pre-occupation with the guides—indeed, in some circles this is known as "field-guide addiction." I hasten to add that field-guide use may certainly be the quickest way to identify the birds; but it is in the long run not the best way to learn the birds. My intent is not to find fault with the field guides. I take issue, instead, with the way they are used, and when they are used.

A birder with his field guide goes into the field and finds a bird. Unless it is one of the more common birds in the neighborhood, the birder immediately grabs for the book and wildly leafs through the pages, scanning pictures. When the live bird is matched up with a picture in the book, the birder ticks off that bird on his checklist and goes on. But one wonders if, by playing this game of match-up, that birder learned the bird so as to recognize and identify it a week or a month later.

There is a card game—casino, I think—wherein one lays a seven on a seven, a three on a three, or whatever, and picks up the cards. The kind of birding just described is not dissimilar. Our birder is matching pictures with live birds, and keeping score. When the same bird shows up a week later, the picture-matcher will go through the same process of finding the picture that most closely resembles the bird in the tree, again happily checking the bird off his list. What has been learned, as familiarity with the book increases, is where to find the picture of that bird quickly!

One of the side effects of "match-up learning" is that after finding the particular bird in the field guide, the birder then "sees" marks or characters on the live bird that are/were not actually present. "Reading" marks onto an unfamiliar bird—given the fact that the sighting is usually a case of "Here it is, there it was!"—is very common.

Because of space limitations, only selected ages, plumages and subspecies are shown in any field guide. Sometimes the selections are not all one could wish. For example, as of the time this is written [January 1981], no picture is given in any of the field guides of the juvenile Semipalmated Sandpiper. Thus, should a birdwatcher in late summer or early fall see one (and almost all Semipalmateds would be juveniles after August, inasmuch as being precocial, the birds would have molted from the downy young feathers they were born with into juvenile plumage by early July, by which time the adults would already be flying south) and refer to the field guide, the influence of the latter is so strong that the birder's own description of the bird he is actually seeing is likely to become distorted and resemble the only picture he has to go by, that of a feather-worn, gray-backed bird! But what he is looking at is the juvenile, with its very dark back, every feather fresh and new. And that, whatever the field guide depicts, is what he should describe.

Birders should also be aware that up to this time all field guides on North American birds have been produced in the eastern part of the country. Because the authors/illustrators use skins to describe and to paint from which have been collected, apparently, in the East—and never, seemingly, in the West—problems are encountered in the West. One example: The Bar-tailed Godwit.

As depicted in every field guide except one, this species presents a flashing white rump. This is the subspecies *Limosa lapponica lapponica* that drops in on the East Coast from Europe. On the West Coast, where the subspecies *Limosa lapponica baueri* ventures from northern Asia and from its breeding grounds (which include north-western Alaska), the bird has no white rump, merely white or whitish upper tail coverts on the essentially brownish tail. Peterson's western field guide indeed presents a perfect painting of *L. lapponica baueri*, but his text inexplicably reads, "In any plumage, shows white rump and white tail crossed by narrow dark bars." And sure enough "a white rump" is all too often included in write-ups of the rare Bar-tailed Godwit in southern California!

Pictures and text can taint your notes. Of course, field-guide descriptions and portrayals can be of inestimable assistance—if consulted at the proper times. Used at the wrong times, innocently enough, they can very easily lead you astray.

How many of us can accurately describe in writing—or in a

drawing, for that matter—any uncommon bird in our own region? Try it. Just try it and discover how difficult it really is. Aside from the critical field marks suggested in the field guides, what does the bird really look like to you, what is your "feel" for it, and how may it be distinguished from another bird similar to it in size and color? Most of us, without some practice, would not even come close to a true representation.

Could one hope to pass a final exam without having taken notes on the lectures? Merely reading the textbooks is ordinarily not enough. As good and as helpful as the field guides may be—and they are indeed continually being improved—in truth and in fact our almost total reliance on them and our almost universal lack of note-taking in the field is astounding.

As one alternative to the match-up game, the traditional British way of birding is to leave the books and pictures at home. A pencil and note-pad are carried instead. This practice makes for a more careful and critical examination of the bird being observed and for more accurate notes, untainted by a picture in a book.

It is not my intent either to downgrade the importance of the field guides in common usage today, or to demean those that produce them or those that use them. The thrust, rather, of this article is to put into proper perspective the use of the field guide as a learning tool. There is nothing wrong with carrying with you the field guides, all of them—indeed the more the better—and referring to them in the car. Just don't stare down at a picture of a bird during the precious seconds the live bird is in view. To spend this valuable time looking at a picture in a book after a competent guide identifies a bird can very well drive a birding tour leader up the wall faster than a European Wallcreeper might make the same climb. For they know that birds, even as human beings, are individuals, that the alternate plumage can be very, very broad, and that no single book could possibly present every stage of development, molting and color change in every species.

They know, too, that unfortunately some authors are not up with the "state of the art," and that even if they were there is such a time gap between putting a book together for the printer and actual publication—often years!—that there will be some birding points outmoded before the public has the book in hand.

The experts know also that it has happened that the artist, for one reason or another, has picked up the wrong bird skin and consequently painted the wrong age or the wrong plumage, or, alas, in the case of certain photographic field guides, that even the wrong species of birds has been designated. Somehow mistakes get by printers and editors, and even authors and illustrators.

Birdwatchers should also remember that the discipline of scientific illustration requires that the artist decide, at the expense of the whole, that a wing or the bill, or some other particular part of a bird, be enhanced and highlighted for easy identification purposes. That is, after all, the purpose of a scientific illustrator, and such highlighting provides the obvious benefit of the painted picture over the very chancy, unposed, often ambiguous photograph. Finally there is the problem of reproducing perfect color tone. Although the art of color printing has made quantum leaps in the past few years, and although we must rejoice in its quality in our present-day books, a human being does the painting, a human being matches the colors, and a human being decides "This is it; let's roll the presses." And we human beings are indeed fallible, are we not?

So learn to practice the field techniques of the experts, remembering that a particular bird may never come your way again. Study the live bird, make notes, and only later, back in your car or at home, look at and compare your notes with your books.

This method may, in truth, take somewhat longer; but don't get discouraged. Do it a little at a time, and it does get easier with practice. Your goal should not be to immediately astound your fellows by being the first to identify a strange bird if that means you may not recognize the bird the next time you see it. In the long run you want to know that bird time after time without looking in a book. If one bird gets away, don't let it get you down; keep at it, and you will become a better birder. If, indeed, the bird is very unusual or rare in your area and you write a description, you certainly do not want to write it based upon its picture. The very last thing an expert wants to hear is, "It looked just like the picture in the book."

Notes should be made and kept in logical and systematic sequence for ease of later retrieval. Try to put down the description each time in the same order. Do this by looking for the different parts of the bird in the same sequence. The following is the order hoped for by state rarities committees:

First, describe your impression of the bird after a good look. What is the "feel" you get for it? Is it shy or brassy? Tired and worn or trim and energetic? Study the bird in life for its gestalt, that is, the bird in its entirety. Study its silhouette, its markings, its coloring, its call—if any—its behavior, its habitat. Of course, there will be times when all you are able to see is the underside of a warbler, and you may not note its dorsal surface until the very moment it flies off. But generally speaking, you should look at the whole bird and form an impression of its self, its manner, its condition.

Then describe the specific parts of the bird, beginning with its dorsal surface at the head, the cap, the face—including any eye ring or superciliary—the nape, the back, the rump, the wings and wing coverts, then the flight feathers—primaries and secondaries, and how long the wings come down on the tail—then the top of the tail.

Next describe the ventral or undersurface of the bird, again starting at the head, then the chin, the throat, the breast, the belly, the vent area, the underwing, the undertail coverts, and the underside of the tail itself.

Then describe the soft parts, that is, the bill—its length, color, curvature; the eye; and if possible, the legs and feet. Finally, try to note the chip or call—or was the bird silent?

If two birders are together it makes note-taking easier. One should call out the description while the other writes it. When this is completed, trade places, only this time the written description should be read back so that the former writer, now the observer, can agree or disagree with length of tail, coloration of back, or whatever. If the bird is indeed a rare bird for that area, this will give the new sight record more credibility.

Compare the identification with the books only after the notes are made. Having the book at hand during note-taking will only interfere with the entire process. Many possibly good and valid records have been tarnished because the observer consulted the book before finishing the notes. As a result, the description often is that of the picture, not of the actual live bird seen.

Of course, if you are an able photographer, and if you happen to have a camera handy, and if the sun is right, and if the bird is cooperative, by all means take its picture in full, living color. One good picture is worth a thousand words; but, of course, for a rarities committee, it would still be helpful to write a description.

In summary, study the pictures in the field guides and digest the text—at home, before you go birding. After you've been birding, go through the book and make comparisons of text and picture with your written description. Carry a small pad for note-taking, particularly for a troublesome bird you cannot identify readily. Scribbling an abbreviated ID will help you to remember it. Pick a birding buddy who knows the territory and/or knows more about the birds you are after than you do—and listen attentively, taking notes.

With just a little practice this British method will become as habitual as the old field-guide method used to be, and very soon you will find that in the field you are using the books much less frequently. And you will find yourself seeing much more.

Certainly, if you feel this new way of learning the birds is just too much of a chore, you may adopt merely a part of it by carring your field guide in your hip pocket and simply jotting down some descriptive notes on the page where you find the bird's picture. That way your notes will always go where you go, and you will find yourself seeing and jotting down something new and different about that bird each time you look it up.

Of course, there is nothing wrong with going birding just to enjoy the birding, but I can testify that there is a great depth to the kind of birdwatching I've been describing. The more you know about the birds, the more you want to know, and indeed the more there is to know; and the more you know about the birds, the more you will enjoy birding.

Enough, for now, of this talking about it. Bins hangin' from me neck, pad and pencil in me pocket (field guides safely stashed in the car), I'm off to do a bit o' birding meself!

(Publication by the National Geographic Society of *Field Guide to the Birds of North America* after this was in print has gone a long way toward correcting many of the faults found in earlier field guides.)

2.
The Joy of Birding the Northeast

WE ARE STANDING on the deck of "Squid's" lobster boat in the Bay of Fundy. The wind-driven rain pelts our faces. The cold Atlantic waters reflect the somber gray-green sky. But this is only the second day of rain in two weeks of birding the Canadian Islands and the Northeast.

A Parasitic Jaeger harasses a Herring Gull into disgorging its meal. The jaeger swoops down, nabs the booty, and flees, disappearing as it appeared, jet-like. Every few minutes we flush a raft of black-capped, white-rumped Greater Shearwaters, fork-tailed Common Terns and the giant-sized Great Black-backed Gulls pass smoothly overhead.

We are close now to Moore Ledge, known to fishermen and birders as a plankton garden. The rain strikes with such force it is impossible to keep our binoculars dry. To avoid a frustrating blur we must wipe both ends of the glasses just as we raise them to observe a bird. We had come aboard armed with wads of paper towels and toilet tissue. When these are soaked useless, we set up what we call our "toilet paper dryer" around the hot vertical exhaust pipe just inside Squid's cabin door. From then on we scurry fore and aft between the drying paper and the wet deck, hurrying lest we miss a good bird.

The majority of Common Eiders are still in summer eclipse plumage, but a few are beginning to come back into courtship dress

25

with a bit of green at the back of the head. (All ducks, except Ruddy and Masked, stay in the same plumage throughout the year until in summer they undergo the eclipse-plummage change for approximately six weeks.) There are clusters of Common Puffin, many still wearing the striking red front on the lobster-claw bill even as winter approaches. By contrast the sedate Razorbills and some Black Guillemots are still essentially black and white, appearing as things out of the olden days, out of pre-color television.

Someone yells, "Whale ahoy!" And the chase is on to stay as close as possible to a thirty-foot long hump-backed whale, which comes up to blow first on one side of our boat and then on the other—an awesome beast that would be frightening were it not so obviously peace-loving and friendly.

And even as we play hide-and-seek with the whale, close by are many white-rumped Leach's Storm-Petrels, pelagic butterflies, and here and there, as if on their toes, the wave-dancing Wilson's Storm-Petrels—while against the dark sky, white-bellied Northern Gannets soar majestically.

Now from far over the choppy waters appears a great woolly milling cloud of Red Phalaropes, perhaps as many as five thousand of them, wheeling and turning together, then skeining off swiftly one after the other, into single-stranded threads miles long; and finally, almost as one, they all drop to the rain-splattered ocean to feed on droplets of oil filled with fattening plankton—prior to starting their long voyage south.

Now we are on Otter Point, a small spit of land reaching out into the Atlantic Ocean off the northernmost coast of Maine. It is early morning, and we kick at patches of fog as we saunter toward the high cliff. Peering over the edge, we gaze down on a billowy carpet of gray fog. Unlike the larger points and many of the islands hereabouts, there is no ancient and venerable lighthouse to conjure up the high adventure of long-gone sailing ships lost in the gloom. But just as romantic is the sound of the buoy bells, welling up above the hypnotic music of the sea breaking on the rocks below.

We are looking especially for migrating warblers, searching avidly for movement in the stunted trees and shrubs—and on the ground too, in hopes of a Mourning or even a Connecticut. There are flurries of excitement when a good bird is discovered.

Someone yells, "Black-and-white!"

All binoculars swing around to pinpoint the tiny bird making its way nervously down the branch of a tree; probing, nipping, hurriedly creeping on.

"Flesh-colored fists—another Blackpoll!"

"Here's a Red-eyed Vireo."

Cape Mays and Northern Parulas are soon "trash birds." By noon we have "bagged" many fine species, including thirteen warblers alone.

We are surrounded on three sides by the sea, and on each side a bell buoy sounds its double tones, each bell tolling in a way that is distinct from the others. Thus, a fisherman out in the fog can determine by the buoy sounds the position of his boat and its heading. The alternate tolling and clanging of the bells creates a remarkably beautiful carillon, the tones lingering in the heavy air. This is indeed an integral part of the normal approaching and receding litany of the sea on this storm-tossed northeast coast.

Aware of this musical phenomenon, from time to time we stand silent, listening. There is a gnawing loneliness one feels when wrapped in fog, anyway—an eeriness that quiets one's soul. It is a strange and awesome experience, and for the moment birding ceases.

But only for a moment.

Someone shouts, "Black-capped and Boreal Chickadees together!" And the spell is broken—giving way, in that instant, to an even more magical game.

BIRD LOG

NOTE: *The following birds were spotted by Mr. Bernstein on the birding trip(s) described in this chapter. They are in the order they were sighted.*

BAY OF FUNDY, CANADA:
Parasitic Jaeger, *Stercorarius parasiticus*
Herring Gull, *Larus argentatus*
Greater Shearwater, *Puffinus gravis*
Common Tern, *Sterna hirundo*
Great Black-backed Gull, *Larus marinus*
Common Eider, *Somateria mollisima*
Common Puffin, *Fratercula arctica*, also known as Atlantic Puffin
Razorbill, *Alca torda*
Black Guillemot, *Cepphus grylle*
Leach's Storm-Petrel, *Oceanodroma leucorhoa*
Wilson's Storm-Petrel, *Oceanites oceanicus*
Gannet, or Northern Gannet, *Morus bassanus*
Red Phalarope, *Phalaropus fulicarius*

OTTER POINT, MAINE:
Black-and-white Warbler, *Mniotilta varia*
Blackpoll Warbler, *Dendroica striata*
Red-eyed Vireo, *Vireo olivaceus*
Cape May Warbler, *Dendroica tigrina*
Northern Parula, *Parula americana*
Black-capped Chickadee, *Parus atricapillus*
Boreal Chickadee, *Parus hudsonicus*

3.
Finding the Great Gray Owl.

THE LATE July sun is about to set here in the Yosemite high country; the shadows lengthen, and the chill air quickly pervades all as if poured from a bucket. Here at eight thousand feet, where the soggy meadows are ringed with quaking aspen and lodgepole pine and red fir towering beyond belief into the clean-washed sky, is the home of the great Gray Owl of the Sierras. That is why I am here...again.

For years I have been dropping in on Yosemite, just because I happen to be passing nearby, on the outside chance of finding the largest of our North American owls. Seeking out the Great Gray can be an all-engrossing illness. And there is but one cure for this fever.

Oh, I had been assured time and again that the huge and yellow-eyed predator is so unafraid it might easily be discovered asleep and unconcerned on a snag at the edge of any clearing; or, diurnal, after all, it might easily be sighted moving heavily with slow wingbeats, close overhead, hunting, or, indeed, feeding on its prey—a mouse, a shrew, a small bird in a tree along the rim of almost any meadow in this part of the mountain range. Rich Stallcup had told me tales of taking its picture while standing just a few feet away!

Such stories keep the adrenalin flowing; they make one envious and eager; and they elevate a few degrees the determination of birders who have for years wandered, wet-footed, cold, and weary, about the remote openings in the forest of this wild area, hoping somehow to stumble over this most elusive bird.

I am very carefully and quietly making my way around the periphery of my third meadow today, checking through my binoculars, before I make each move, every branch on every tree. (Learning to hunt for snipers in the infantry was not a total loss.) This will be my last round for the day: Total darkness will blanket everything soon.

The young coyote that has been following me at a safe distance stops when I stop, the eyes curious but careful to turn away when I try to stare him down. The song of a Western Wood-Pewee rains down on the world from the top of a red fir while the Red-breasted Nuthatch sounds his toy horn, and the Steller's Jays raucously proclaim this intruder's presence. I startle a doe with her fawn into springlike action. Then, just as suddenly, they return to their browsing, the doe warily watching me with her enormous, glistening "black-olive" eyes.

Tired now and frustrated in the gathering dusk, but unwilling to leave, still hoping to catch a glimpse of the owl in flight—if only in silhouette—I sit on a log and wait. Suddenly a young man appears, making quick long strides across the meadow.

John Lovio is his name, he tells me. He is a student and an assistant to Jon Winter, a northern California biologist-birder, who is conducting—would you believe it—a Great Gray Owl study! He saw a Great Gray just an hour ago!

I am elated. "May I join you?"

"Sure. Haven't talked to anyone for ten days!"

He has been marking the roosting trees of the big owl and collecting and marking the positions of its pellets in different meadows. When the study is completed, the numbers of pellets and their positions would be computerized, and total population could be determined.

On a dead run I accompany him through several miles of forest trail to a meadow at a higher elevation, so he may confirm that the owl he saw last night in the higher meadow is not the same owl he saw an hour ago in another meadow. However, there is no response to his perfect owl calling. With the aid of a tiny flashlight, back down we go in almost total darkness, my footsteps in his.

Later, over a shared supper, Lovio reveals how Jon Winter taught him to find the Great Gray.

"Robins go, *Cluck! Cluck! Beep! Beep!*" Winter told him. "When a robin drops its *Cluck! Cluck!* and goes *Beep! Beep! Beep! Beep!* persistently, that means Great Gray Owl."

It is common knowledge among birders that especially during nesting season small birds will go to herioc lengths to drive away large predators. (In my mind there is forever imprinted a picture of a hummingbird scolding brutally and chasing off a Golden Eagle. Incongruous sight!) I have heard too that small birds will mob the smaller owls and hawks, and that large birds will mob the larger predators. If the robin is the only bird in the area big and brave enough to have a confrontation with a Great Gray, then Winter's method should work. Why not? Listen for the robin! I can scarcely wait for morning to test the method.

I awake to the loud drumming on hollow trees of the Black-backed (Three-toed) Woodpeckers, the tinkling of Dark-eyed (Oregon) Juncos and the long melodious phrases of Cassin's Finches, more bubbly perhaps, but not too different from the gurgling warble of the Purple Finches I heard down in the valley at Crane Flats.

It is 10:00 a.m. by the time Lovio marks all his specimens, brings his log-book up to date, and is ready to move out. I could have left without him, but it is always worth waiting for someone who knows the territory. It makes a "good possibility" almost a "sure thing." Bitter experience has taught me a good birding maxim: There will always be at least two left turns omitted from directions for how to get to a good bird.

At long last we arrive at McGurk Meadow. Scanning the margins with binoculars we find no owl. We move some thirty yards into the trees back of the meadow and make owl noises. Almost immediately we hear a loud and persistent, *Beep! Beep! Beep! Beep!*

"Robins!" I yell in a hoarse whisper.

"Wait and see if it's persistent...It is!"

I am off like a jet, running headlong through the pathless forest, leaping over fallen trees and going around patches of brush too thick to pass through, Lovio right with me, led by the unmistakable and hysterical robin call.

"There's the robin!"

I am looking at a robin that in its excitement can barely manage to stay upright on a branch while vehemently screaming its single epithet again and again and again. Its bill is actually pointing to the giant tawny-gray bird that seems to fidget uncomfortably on its perch only a foot or so out from the trunk and perhaps fifteen feet up in the adjacent pine tree.

We surmise that the owl had been well hidden on its day roost but that our owl-calling flushed it out.

(If the robins are not already on a Great Gray, the success of this "mobbing" method depends on the owl being flushed or at least moved on its roost—by owl-calling, squeaking, or whatever—so the other birds are alerted to its presence.)

Once it moves the robins are harassing it without pity. As we come closer the owl flushes, but only for a short distance. And the robins, with their loud and steady *Beep! Beep!* direct us to it, are after it and indeed pointing to it!

I am easily able to follow the owl, flushing it twice more, and getting a good look at its facial discs, while John goes back to mark the original tree we found it in and to seek out pellets, if any, beneath it. There were none.

I watch the owl finally disappear through the trees, presumably out of robin territory. All is calm again. How simple it all seems.

"Thank you, John, and give my best to Jon Winter." With a spring in my step I make my way out to the highway, laughing aloud each time I hear above me, *Cluck! Cluck! Beep! Beep!*

```
BIRD LOG
NOTE: The following birds were spotted by Mr. Bernstein on the birding
trip(s) described in this chapter. They are in the order they were sighted.
```

YOSEMITE NATIONAL PARK, CALIFORNIA:
Western Wood-Pewee, *Contopus
    sordidulus*
Red-breasted Nuthatch, *Sitta
    canadensis*
Steller's Jay, *Cyanocitta stelleri*
Black-backed (Three-toed)
    Woodpecker, *Picoides arcticus*
Dark-eyed (Oregon) Junco, *Junco
    hyemalis oreganus*
Cassin's Finch, *Carpodacus cassinii*
American Robin, *Turdus migratorius*
Great Gray Owl, *Strix nebulosa*

4.
Some Birds That Got Away.

EVERY BIRDWATCHER has tales of "the bird that got away." Some misadventures are easily shrugged off; others, more traumatic, can tug at the memory for years. The emergence of a string of birding hotlines or bird alerts across the country has added much to the storehouse, and the birding community is, in fact, awash with tales of birders striving mightily to reach the site of a "record" bird, only to miss it because of a breakfast stop. Or a wrong turn. Or simply because the bird, though "it was here just a half hour ago," is not around right now (is probably on its way to another continent by now)!

Every birdwatcher also remembers a memorable bird as being precisely where it was last seen—and in his/her mind it will indeed be there forever. I will not soon forget what Elizabeth Copper, an excellent birder, on a trip to the Salton Sea, said about Guy McCaskie (Southern Pacific Coast Regional Editor for *American Birds* and more than avid, a virulent birder): "I'm so relieved we found this Ruff. Had I gone back and told Guy we hadn't found it, he'd have said, 'Why, hell, it's right there, over the bank, just thirty feet from the road, right where I left it! How could you miss it?"

Recalling a hurtful or embarrassing episode may open an old wound, but, tell the truth and shame the devil, finding every bird you go after exactly where it is supposed to be would take all the fun out of birdwatching, and the hobby would go into rapid decline—as would baseball if every batter that went to the plate hit the ball out of the park. Here are some of my own strikeouts:

AMERICAN WOODCOCK

To forearm myself against the missed-bird syndrome I have for years been keeping myself in shape for the catastrophe of missing "the big one" by regularly missing the common American Woodcock. Yes, the "very common (in some parts of the country, in some months of the year, when I am not present)," brown, long-billed woodcock. I have conscientiously sought it, and several times have almost been rewarded, in six different states. The "almost rewarded" means I have been privileged to view the rear end and tail feathers of this, for me, elusive bird on at least three different occasions. Indeed, I feel by now an expert on the bird's nether parts, but alas, to check it off on my life list is still out of the the question. I want to look a woodcock in the eye—well, I'd settle for anywhere in the face.

Inasmuch as it eats ground worms, the species prefers moist, low, leaf-covered ground under a low canopy of trees, so the sun won't get in. It remains silent and motionless (not even an eyelid blinks) when man is about, and—I am given to understand—it looks so much like the dead leaves it forages in it is all but impossible to see on the ground. It will wait almost until stepped on before it flushes in a loud flurry of feathers, up through the trees, and then turns right (or occasionally left, I suppose, for all I know), never to be seen again.

I am told they are easy to locate during their mating time in early spring when the male flies high into the air and spirals his way down toward earth again, all the while showering the awaiting females watching below with the most exotic caroling. Due to spring commitments in the West I have never witnessed this avian mating spectacle.

In the fall of 1968 my wife, Elsie, and I were slowly making our way along a path in the Laughing Brook Nature Center in Massachusetts. We were as hushed and awed as the surroundings were silent and solemn: we had discovered what to us was an open-air cathedral. Beside the path flowed a tinkling stream that divided a great bed of gold and brown leaves to either side. Suddenly the tranquility was shattered by the loud and frenzied beating of feathers, and away the bird went through the forest. We saw enough of it to know it was indeed a woodcock, but felt at the time—and still do—it was three-quarters of a bird away from our life lists.

Again, in the fall of 1971 while on a visit to long-time birding friend, Myra McNally, at Lake Geneva, Wisconsin, I was escorted to a nearby marsh where the slippery muck I was sliding through and a slap in the face by a willow branch prevented me from gleaning more than a rear-end view of a flying-away woodcock.

Another fall, in Acadia National Park, Maine, where Will Russell and I sloshed through an alder swale (they say the surest place to find 'em) I flushed a member of the species which promptly flew through the trees, turned right and, of course, disappeared before we could make it out to the roadway.

I've missed the bird entirely on several other occasions. In the fall of 1974, I think it was, Pat Murphy, another long-time birding friend and writer about birds, took Elsie and me out to a small town in Ohio along the Muskingum River, where the late P.O. Hart—"The Walker," as Pat referred to him in her columns—knew there were woodcocks. I was directed to walk through a rather dense wild area for several acres, The Walker having assured me he had never not kicked out a woodcock from this woods. When I came out some time later, covered with stick-tights and well brushed with what felt like nettles, The Walker said, well it had indeed been an extremely dry year, and this was the "first time in history" the long-billed bird had not been flushed from the premises. So I felt at least I had made history.*

Steeer-i-i-i-ke One!

THE IMPOSSIBLE BUFF-COLLARED NIGHTJAR

July 4, 1975: By 8:00 A.M. we are well out in the high desert in our birding buddy Ernie Abeles's new car, driving east on a two-lane

---

*Having also sought the woodcock on several other occasions in Ohio, West Virginia and Tennessee, I finally saw the bird (No. 654 on my life list) on April 15, 1981, in a marsh near Parkersburg, West Virginia.

highway out of Douglas, Arizona, headed for a rumored Buff-collared Nightjar in Guadalupe Canyon.

Spotting birds along the way, we drive at a leisurely pace, enjoying the clean-washed desert air. It rained last night, but this morning one would think the countryside had merely been covered with dew. It disappears that fast. And, of course, this time of year southeast Arizona gets at least an hour of rain every afternoon or evening, anyway. Nothing unusual about that.

As per directions, we turn off onto a gravel road, which soon becomes dirt and narrows as we make our way toward the border with Mexico. Almost immediately we find ourselves in "remote" desert. We pass, in several miles of travel, but one lonely farmhouse, and after that there seems to be no link to "civilization."

We approach a fork in the road where we are supposed to branch to the left. Just as we reach the fork, however, the road drops down, and very suddenly there is almost at our front wheels a river of mud, which moves from our left out of a streambed directly across the road. It is too late to stop. I yell for Ernie to tromp on the accelerator, hoping we can get through to the other side. At the very midpoint, out of concern for his new car, Ernie's toe eases up on the accelerator, the wheels lose all traction, and we stop. And it is impossible to get any movement out of the new car, either forward or backward.

On getting out to assess our situation, I find myself in gluey mud almost to my knees. It is well above the midpoint on the hubcaps. Quickly we try the usual things in attempting to free ourselves— diverting the mud floe to one side, away from the wheels: using a piece of cardboard for a shovel; gathering rocks and dry tree limbs and positioning them under the tires. Nothing helps. We are hopelessly mired.

By this time Ernie is very upset about his new car, but on this Independence Day weekend we realize there may not be another car along this miserable pathway for several days. We lock the car, slip our binoculars on, and, taking along a canteen of water and a sack of food, start the long hike back to the main highway.

When we finally reach the farmhouse passed earlier, our worst fears are realized—there is no one home. Everyone is, of course, in town, meeting old friends, stocking up on groceries, having a beer, enjoying the carnival, and waiting for the fireworks display after dark. We walk on.

In sight of the highway we wince as a car going toward Douglas whizzes by at around ninety miles an hour. Just as we reach the highway, very conscious now of the sun's intensity, a very large, very old car comes roaring down the highway and does not slow down after seeing our outstretched thumbs. Then Ernie proves his true worth. He remembers and screams out the Spanish word for "Help!"

The car stops. One of the nine members of the tightly packed auto comprehends enough English so we are understood. We are dropped off in Douglas and pay them with a tank of gasoline. An auto club tow truck returns us to the site of "the mud floe massacre," and pulls the car out together with half the mud in Arizona.

Had we been pulled out on the side that led to Guadalupe Canyon we just might have continued with our original mission. But headed back toward the main highway, and whole again, though frustrated, we mush on to the Southwest Research Station at Cave Creek, where that night a severe lightning storm displays for us the most dramatic Fourth of July either of us has ever experienced. And Guadalupe Canyon, that would have to wait for another day.

July 19, 1977: We are on an ABA Weekend in Arizona and already have some of the most glorious birding ever under our belts. Now at dusk we are headed in a caravan down a familiar highway east out of Douglas for an attempt at—guess what—a Buff-collared Nightjar in Guadalupe Canyon! This time we're sure we'll make it. As if on cue (I say the canyon heard I was coming), the sky clouds up, and it starts to rain. Immediately the roadway becomes so slick cars are slipping and sliding completely out of control, and we are unable to continue.

We backtrack and set up in a motel in Douglas to wait out the rain. But it rains all night. A scouting party is sent out twice to test the road surface for an attempt the following morning. It is impossible. Next morning the Guadalupe Canyon trip is abandoned, and we move on instead to Cave Creek's South Fork where as luck would have it we find a Rufous-capped Warbler. It is a more than fair trade-off. But that canyon is still waiting for us.

You just can't get there from here! Steeer-i-i-i-ke Two!

May 23, 1978 (the fifth day of a tour of Attu in the Aleutian Islands; from my unpublished *Attu Diary*): Amidst the merriment of studying my seventeenth life bird on this trip we get on the radio at 6:00 P.M. to report the Black-tailed Godwit, which is still in Henderson Marsh. We are weary from bounding over tundra, hiking over the mountains, pushing through springy young willows, and sloshing through the marsh since early morning; and the thought of heading for the gym and some rest is comforting.

But all on Attu is life-or-death emergency, overwhelming surprise or heartrending disappointment; and expectations are as fickle as the weather, which changes from sunshine to sleet and snow to rain and hail and back to sunshine every fifteen minutes.

Joe Taylor comes on the air, and we hear his gruff bass voice tell of seeing two, perhaps three, Hawfinches. Jim Tucker had found them just outside of the abandoned Loran station at Murder Point, where Taylor, Tucker, and five others were bunking. Hawfinches! The word rings out over the marsh.

Davis Finch spits into the microphone. "On our way! Over and out." Aware of how spooky Hawfinches are, we do not dawdle. It is almost ten miles from where we are to Murder Point, and we alternate running with a fast walk the entire distance. Davis is out front, but when he reaches the road that leads to the old gymnasium he leaves to advise those still "at home" of the new find. My tent mate, Tom Kent, and I scurry along together. Tom, in his most professional manner, several times suggests that "We ought to pace ourselves, I really think we ought to pace ourselves."

I don't answer him. I can't even talk. This is the start of what has become known as the Hawfinch Death March. Ray Hannikman says he is going to have T-shirts made with that wording printed across the front. Noble Proctor says that in the center should be pictured the sole of a human foot. And I add, "Yes—cracked into little pieces." I pretend I can go on forever. The truth is, my left ankle is killing me (something I have not felt since World War II), my left arch feels like a sharp knife has been pushed into it, and I am conscious of mean things being done to the soles of my feet and all the toes.

At approximately the six-mile marker Noble jogs past us as if we are standing still. But this only spurs us on. Wincing each time I put a foot down, I finally decide to resort to what I think of as Far East mysticism (which I know, really, nothing of), saying to myself over and over again, "My feet don't hurt. I'm not running on feet; I am flying on wings!"

It works. My "wings" get me there. Tom times us and swears we make it in just over one hour, probably almost true. Here on Attu I often feel I am back in the combat infantry where time is critical to survival and where physical pain is buried under layers of—well, more important priorities.

As we finally reach the old building at Murder Point I see that up ahead on the gravel road Noble is talking to Joe. Art Clark stands near a shed on the side of the mountain to the right. I yell up to Art, "Where's the birds?" Art, turtle-like, pulls his head down into his shoulders, his arms extended to the sides, palms up. He doesn't know! My heart sinks.

"The birds, where are the birds?" I ask of Noble and Joe.

Noble raises one eyebrow and snorts. "They don't know. They flew away." Tom asks, "In which direction?" Joe says. "Oh, we don't know."

Joe then explains that Jim had been returning from a hike around Casco Bay, had in fact been looking in a book at a picture of a Hawfinch, had looked up and seen a live one on a nearby post being harassed by the nesting Lapland Longspurs and Snow Buntings. Jim had called out Joe, his wife, Helen, and Larry Balch and Barbara Sullivan, who were all staying at the old Loran station, and they had gotten a look at a single Hawfinch. Joe says that after perhaps a minute it flew off and was not seen again. They had then returned to their interrupted dinner.

Joe had indeed got on the radio at 6:30 to report its disappearance, but by then we were spread out along the route to Murder Point. Had we heard his call-off announcement, it would not have mattered; we should still have gone on to the area where the Hawfinch was last seen and mounted a desperation search for it.

Bill and Harriet Davidson, having been alerted by Davis, appear, learn the bitter truth, and resignedly turn and head back for the gym. Bill is barely able to walk. Enter Dick Brownstein wildly pedaling his bicycle over the bumpy road with his one good leg, the other stuck out like a long curbfinder. The chase music accompanying the Keystone Cops silent films comes to mind.

Rich Stallcup and Ray Hannikman (having finally given up watching the Black-tailed Godwit to come see the Hawfinch) arrive, as does Davis, limping painfully and just barely able, it seems, to crawl up the side of the mountain and to lie there hoping to catch sight of the flown bird or birds. From his perch he does his best to organize search parties to scout the entire area.

Next comes Harold Axtell, looking very pale and exhausted, and bedecked in his fine green $240 "guaranteed leakproof" rain suit that leaks. I am told Nick Greene and John Keenleyside are far out at Alexai Point and so, fortunately, have missed the Death March. Rich and Ray comb the upper reaches of the mountainside, Noble and Jim walk out to the very end of the point. Tom, thoroughly disgusted with the misadventure and just able to place one foot ahead of the other, heads slowly toward the gym.

I also am sick at heart. I hate to miss a bird. I may never make it back to Attu. I lie back on the soft tundra for a while, cooling down, then make a couple of maneuvers up the side of the mountain and around the old sheds there. Finally, telling Davis I will check all structures up the road, I start for the gym. Slowly. Slowly.

I meander in my trek back so that I may carefully investigate each broken-down cabin and all the rusty rubble around it. I still hope to find the Hawfinch. Alas, none of us finds it again. But we might have. The Bean Goose flies overhead, and a white male Snowy Owl and many Lapland Longspurs and Snow Buntings.

It is 10:30 P.M. when I finally reach the gym. The two lanterns are lit, and the cavernous gym is again invested with an eeriness which only lantern light can evoke. A pot of stew has been kept warm. I have not eaten since the granola bar and the can of sardines at lunchtime, more than ten hours ago. The stew is delicious and tastes as if made with fresh vegetables, though we know it is "from the envelope into the pot."

Most of our group have turned in, some too tired to eat anything. A few weary stragglers enter in the eerie lantern light, eat in silence and vanish into their tents. There is no talk; all is very quiet.

Now I "feel" my feet for the first time in hours. I remove my boots and socks. The toes on both feet are plastered with congealed blood.

There is a brand new raw place on my left ankle where the skin has simply worn away, and there are blisters under the blisters over the bruises on the soles of my feet. Tonight, in cold water, I bathe them; tomorrow morning is soon enough to do patching.

This is the quietest night we have known in the gym. And it is not the physical problems—after such a devastating hike we did not get our bird; it is the disappointment that galls and hushes us all.

May 24, 1978 (the sixth day of the tour): It is a tragicomic day indeed. With but two or three exceptions, everyone camped out in this icebox of a gym is either hopping along on one leg, limping painfully, or mincing very gingerly around the gym doin' "The Attu Shuffle."

Boxes of band-aids are used and acres of moleskin, and many a boot is worn this morning without being laced up. Richy pulls two pairs of wool socks over each bandaged foot and stuffs them into a pair of tennis shoes. Davis presents himself wearing a rubber boot on the left to ease the pain of a pulled Achilles tendon and a leather boot on the right foot to lessen the pain of severe stone bruising.

We all share to some degree in the aftershock of the now-celebrated "Hawfinch Death March." But this is another day, and we are just as anxious to get out there and see what the "night flight" brought to our little island from Siberia this morning as we were yesterday morning. The "Boulevard of Broken Feet," just as soon as we get a report of a good bird, will become the "Indianapolis Race Track" once again.

Steeer-i-i-i-ke Three, Yer Out!

ß

Not every bird walk ends in triumphant elation; there are just enough heartbreaks to keep the sport remarkably interesting. And the joy of birding includes both the disappointments and the surprises.

BIRD LOG

NOTE: *The following birds were spotted by Mr. Bernstein on the birding trip(s) described in this chapter. They are in the order they were sighted.*

CAVE CREEK, DOUGLAS, ARIZONA:
Rufous-capped Warbler, *Basileutorus rufifrons*

ATTU ISLAND, ALEUTIAN ISLANDS, ALASKA:
Black-tailed Godwit, *Limosa limosa*
Bean Goose, *Anser fabalis*
Snowy Owl, *Nyctea scandiaca*
Lapland Longspur, *Calcarius lapponicus*
Snow Bunting, *Plectrophenax nivalis*

5.

The Making of a Hot Spot.

TO FIND AND SEE an array of birds in one area is a birdwatcher's dream. Birders will travel through early-morning darkness, drive all night, even journey great distances to reach such a place. There are many well-known hot spots across the continent—Cape May, the Everglades, Point Pelee, to name only three. But how are heretofore unsuspected hot spots discovered? And how is the word of their existence spread?

In October 1980—a good month for rarities on the West Coast, where, as contrasted to the Eastern Seaboard, we are still discovering new prime birding areas—I had the good fortune of accompanying Jon Dunn and Will Russell on a trip to just such a place. Will, a principal in a birding tour agency, had never birded here before. Both Jon and I were anxious to show off "our area," just fifty miles north of Los Angeles via I-5 (Golden State Freeway) and State Highway 14 (Antelope Valley Freeway)—the Antelope Valley.

Its time had come. 1980 had produced, besides the expected birds of the high desert, an abundance of eastern warblers, a Hudsonian Godwit, many Black Terns at the marsh, and a few days later two Arctic Terns over the lake! Surely stuff a birder's dreams are made of.

And from my personal logbook some of my own memories:

April 17, 1970. Barrel Springs Road. Bright morning
sun...juniper and the strong odor of sage...the eager looks on
the faces around me...the wild chase over loose sand, from
bush to bush. I will never forget the wild excitement upon
catching sight of a thin gray bird—my first Leconte's Thrasher!

Until the end of the 1960s the extent of any birding in the Antelope
Valley, either individually or in organized groups, was a single field
trip each year to Littlerock Dam. After all, despite an elevation of
2,500 feet to 3,000 feet, it is part of the great Mojave Desert, and aside
from the "crazy" roadrunner, what birds would live there?

By 1971, John Dunn, Kimball Garrett and others of their generation
(the younger set) were birding this high desert "seriously," meaning at
regular intervals, discovering the best birding spots, and regularly
astounding the older birding community with their finds.

November 27, 1971. 150th W. and Avenue J. It is bitterly cold
and windy. We walk through a flock of dirty gray sheep that
loudly bleat and blah and scatter wildly on our approach. The
brown alfalfa stubble is frozen and crunches underfoot. Small
flocks of Water Pipits and Western Meadowlarks stand apart
and feed.

We walk into a flock of hundreds of Horned Larks, and, as
one, they explode into the air. On flushing, they cry a thin
high-pitched double note. We have been walking into such
flocks and chasing them for over two hours. My fingers are stiff
with cold. The nose on my good friend Hank Brodkin's ruddy
face, it appears, has turned blue.

Again we flush the Horned Larks, and once more, as a single
body, they wheel off and finally settle a few hundred yards
away. But this time one bird at the outer edge of the flock calls
Kidl-kidl!

"Don't lose that bird! Stay with it!"

We run and we run, and finally are in position to set up the
telescope. We cheer for my first Chestnut-collared Longspur,
benumbed conquerors warmed only by our ecstasy.

Traffic and smog are left behind on this day of anticipated revelation for Will Russell, and by 7:00 we are at the Lake Palmdale overlook watching a Common Loon far below us and picking out the Tree from the Violet-green Swallows coursing overhead. The sky is overcast. The air is clear and cold. We must hurry; there is a lot to show.

We drive east on Palmdale Boulevard, past available motels—always a plus for possible birding tours—out past the juniper fields, through the brown foothills covered with Mojave yucca and on to the broad vistas of creosote bush studded with venerable Joshua trees reaching thirty feet toward heaven, like ancient menorahs that have borne witness to history for a long, long time.

We pull up at a familiar wash at 149th E and Avenue Q where there is a good stand of old cottonwoods. In the greasewood clumps are sparrows; fat, orange-billed White-crowneds, *gambelli* being our wintering race; the very small pale Brewer's; a few of the harlequin-faced Sage with their black tails; and a Vesper, large and streaked on the breast.

Deeper in the wash we scare up Bewick's Wrens, a Yellow and an Orange-crowned Warbler—bearing the fail-safe, white identifying mark at the bend of the wing (unmentioned in the field guides perhaps because the mark does not appear on all Orange-crowns), and three ghostly Barn Owls that flush a short distance and try to disappear into the foliage of another cottonwood tree, in utter silence.

Mountain Chickadees, a Plain Titmouse, a Downy Woodpecker and a White-breasted Nuthatch are unusual for the Valley. A Cactus Wren loudly stutters out its tattoo.

February 9, 1977. Valyermo. (Just a few miles to the south.)
Having seen but two in my entire lifetime, I am exultant, counting the rusty undertail coverts of one hundred twenty Bohemian Waxwings!

Willy and Jon talk of temperature ranges. How cold does it get? How hot does it get? I tune out. If there are birds to be found, pull on another jacket, peal off a shirt. What's the difference? Within the past year near here were found Bay-breasted, Northern Parula, Blackpoll and Palm Warbers, all vagrants from the east!

The chill air is intoxicating. We let Will kick out across the desert scrub by himself so that he may better absorb the beauty of this quiet, cold, fall habitat. When he returns I ask what he thinks of it.

He says, "Nice."

New Englanders do that to you.

Lake Los Angeles, close-by, is good for wintering birds. We find nearly a thousand American Coots, flotillas of Shoveler, Ruddy, Redhead, Canvasback and Ring-necked Ducks, clusters of Eared and Pied-billed and Western Grebes, Bufflehead and Lesser Scaup, plus the wading Great Blue Herons and Snowy Egrets. "Nice," but still nothing exciting.

June 14, 1978. 145th E and Avenue Q. A brilliant yellow adult male Scott's Oriole calls from a Joshua tree nearby. A pair of LeConte's Thrashers herd their just days-old chicks across a dry streambed and into hiding. Just below the craggy red rock hill on the north side of the highway, we find Verdin, nesting Verdin, recently discovered at the extreme northwest limit of its range!

From Lake Los Angeles we go north to visit our favorite ranch. Back of the barn feed Golden-crowned Sparrows, and sorting through the flock of Dark-eyed Juncos, we find a Gray-headed Junco. Farming here requires irrigation. In earlier days each farm had to build its own water reservoir, a four-sided dirt bank affair. Today these ponds, surrounded by old willows and cottonwoods and locust trees, remain for the benefit of wildlife, especially birds. Each is truly an oasis.

More Barn Owls, then two Black-throated Gray Warblers with their distinctive yellow lores. A male Northern Harrier (Marsh Hawk) is hunting low over the stubble fields. Then, here to spend the winter, a Ferruginous Hawk, white tail flashing, sails overhead. The clear, whitish tail is a quicker identifier, in either the dark or the light phase, than the dark "V" of the thighs, when the bird is in flight. The dark thigh feathering is only markedly present on the adult, anyway. On the adult the rusty color seems mainly confined to the terminal portion of the dorsal or top surface of the tail, the immature being whiter-tailed still.

The hawk sets down on the crossbar of a telephone pole. It perches vertically, as do hawks, with its tail transecting the crossbar it stands on. Nearby, a late-migrating Turkey Vulture also perches on a crossbar. Because it perches horizontally and parallel with the crossbar, as vultures do, the daylight between its tail and the crossbar quickly distinguishes it from a hawk, even at a great distance. (This posture does not always necessarily apply to Turkey Vultures perched or roosting on tree limbs.)

Willy walks out to better study the Ferruge. He returns almost smiling. The sun is warming now. Three wintering Mountain Bluebirds pause on a wire to look us over.

Making a loop, we now race back west on Avenue J, stopping to check the ponds at four different ranches. Added to our list are Song Sparrow, Say's and Black Phoebes, and a Rufous-sided Towhee, unusual hereabouts. Although Nuttall's and Ladder-backed Woodpeckers overlap in their range here, the Nuttall's we find is easy to distinguish by the very thin white lines on the cheeks. Jon finds skulking in the thick foliage around one pond a male Black-throated Blue Warbler, a rarity in California.

March 20, 1979. Quail Lake. (A few miles to the west.) We stand in a very cold wind looking up at a migrating Swainson's Hawk flying with a northbound flock of Turkey Vultures, which this species often does. Beyond the lake extends a carpet of orange California poppies as far as the eye can see. The luxuriant wildflowers, miles and miles of them, can be dazzling in the spring.

Farther west now to the Lancaster sewage treatment ponds. Now we are into a flat, wild area dotted with saltbush. Skittering scross the road is our ground cuckoo, a Greater Roadrunner, with its blue eye shadow and red earrings.

On the water, from atop the dike, the sun has turned the reflection of the burnt-brown hills all pink and gold. At the edge of one basin stand two late Baird's Sandpipers waiting to see which way we move. There are Ring-billed, California, and Bonaparte's Gulls and a few ducks about, but the hundreds of Wilson's and Northern Phalaropes that filled the ponds just a couple of weeks ago are gone.

When we reach a basin recently emptied of water, we find in the rich muck a Greater Yellowlegs, a few Black-bellied Plovers, and both sexes of Pectoral Sandpiper standing side by side. There is a dramatic difference in size. The male is approximately one-quarter or more larger than the female! It can only be compared to the difference in size between the Greater and Lesser Yellowlegs. Barely mentioned, if at all, in the field guides, the greater size of the male seems to be true of species that use the lek (staging ground where males display to attract females) system for mating, including the Ruff, a close relative of the Pectoral Sandpiper.

The treated water, rich in nutrients, is drained into the Edwards Air Force Base marsh, where it is spread for evaporation. The under-surface of this desert ground is too hard to allow the water to permeate into the underground water table.

Hidden in flat terrain, and reached only by forbidding and long-neglected roads, the marsh was easily overlooked. For birdwatching, it was only discovered in 1977 by Fred Heath, at the time a newly-transplanted avid birder from New York. This marsh is unique in that one may approach very close to shorebirds, if one has no great hangup about wet feet.

> *August 16, 1980.* Edwards Marsh. It is extremely hot...the sun-glare off the water is almost blinding...I am thirsty and think next time I must remember to carry water with me. Jerry Johnson and I stand in the warm mucky water studying, as they feed on a sandspit barely twenty-five feet away, a Least, a rare Semipalmated, a Western, a Baird's and a White-rumped Sandpiper—one of each! The White-rumped is a first autumn record for the western United States! Minus the Rufous-necked Sandpiper, we are looking at everything on page 125 of Chan Robbins' *Birds of North America.*

From among the Least and Western Sandpipers and Avocets and Black-necked Stilts, we quickly add a Mountain Plover, with its distinctive white eyebrow over white-rimmed, giant, ripe-olive eyes in a buffy face, and a long-legged Stilt Sandpiper.

Jon is already in the water. Willy has waded in, clad only in shorts, on my advice having left his trousers in the car. I have tarried to watch the traffic in American Bitterns and Black-crowned Night-Herons, when I hear Willy yell, "Chuck, here's a Ruff!"

I dash out over the bank and into the water—shoes, socks, pants, wallet and all—to where Will is standing, his binoculars pointed at the shoreline perhaps fifty feet away. There it is, a female Ruff (called by some a Reeve), and only the second record for the Valley! This is a tawny, elegant shorebird that stands taller and more erect than the long-billed Dowitchers busily feeding around it, even when they nervously stop feeding to look about. Bobbing up and down, they probe deep. The Ruff pick-pick-picks and does not probe.

The Antelope Valley is now a regular stop on Will Russell's tours to Southern California, and in time will be part of other tours to the southern part of the state. But, after all, as a birding hot spot it is still in its infancy; it has only been "seriously" birded for the past ten years!

BIRD LOG

NOTE: *The following birds were spotted by Mr. Bernstein on the birding trip(s) described in this chapter. They are in the order they were sighted.*

ANTELOPE VALLEY, CALIFORNIA:
LeConte's Thrasher, *Toxostoma lecontei*
Water Pipit, *Anthus spinoletta*
Western Meadowlark, *Sturnella neglecta*
Horned Lark, *Eremophila alpestris*
Chestnut-collared Longspur, *Calcarius ornatus*
Common Loon, *Gavia immer*
Tree Swallow, *Tachycineta bicolor*
Violet-green Swallow, *Tachycineta thalassina*
White-crowned Sparrow, *Zonotrichia leucophrys*
Brewer's Sparrow, *Spizella breweri*
Sage Sparrow, *Amphispiza belli*
Vesper Sparrow, *Pooecetes gramineus*
Bewick's Wren, *Thryomanes bewickii*
Yellow Warbler, *Dendroica petechia*
Orange-crowned Warbler, *Vermivora celata*
Barn Owl, *Tyto alba*
Mountain Chickadee, *Parus gambeli*
Plain Titmouse, *Parus inornatus*
Downy Woodpecker, *Picoides pubescens*
White-breasted Nuthatch, *Sitta carolinensis*
Cactus Wren, *Campylorhynchus brunneicapillas*
Bohemian Waxwing, *Bombycilla garrulus*
American Coot, *Fulica americana*
Northern Shoveler, *Anas clypeata*
Ruddy Duck, *Oxyura jamaicensis*
Redhead, *Aythya americana*
Canvasback, *Aythya valisineria*
Ring-necked Duck, *Aythya collaris*
Eared Grebe, *Podiceps nigricollis*
Pied-billed Grebe, *Podilymbus podiceps*
Western Grebe, *Aechmophorus occidentalis*
Bufflehead, *Bucephala albeola*
Lesser Scaup, *Aythya affinis*
Great Blue Heron, *Ardea herodias*
Snowy Egret, *Egretta thula*
Scott's Oriole, *Icterus parisorum*
Verdin, *Auriparis flaviceps*

Golden-crowned Sparrow, *Zonotrichia atricapilla*
Dark-eyed Junco, *Junco hyemalis*
Dark-eyed Junco (gray-headed race), *Junco hyemalis caniceps*
Black-throated Gray Warbler, *Dendroica nigrescens*
Northern Harrier (Marsh Hawk), *Circus cyaneus*
Ferruginous Hawk, *Buteo regalis*
Turkey Vulture, *Cathartes aura*
Mountain Bluebird, *Sialia currocoides*
Song Sparrow, *Melospiza melodia*
Say's Phoebe, *Sayornis saya*
Black Phoebe, *Sayornis nigricans*
Rufous-sided Towhee, *Pipilo erythrophthalmus*
Nuttall's Woodpecker, *Picoides nutallii*
Black-throated Blue Warbler, *Dendroica caerulescens*
Ladder-backed Woodpecker, *Picoides scalaris*
Swainson's Hawk, *Buteo swainsoni*
Greater Roadrunner, *Geococcyx californianus*
Baird's Sandpiper, *Calidris bairdii*
Ring-billed Gull, *Larus delawarensis*
California Gull, *Larus californicus*
Bonaparte's Gull, *Larus philadelphia*
Greater Yellowlegs, *Tringa melanoleuca*
Black-bellied Plover, *Pluvialis squatarola*
Pectoral Sandpiper, *Calidris melanotos*
Semipalmated Sandpiper, *Calidris pusilla*
Western Sandpiper, *Calidris mauri*
White-rumped Sandpiper, *Calidris fuscicollis*
Least Sandpiper, *Calidris minutilla*
American Avocet, *Recurvirostra americana*
Black-necked Stilt, *Himantopus mexicanus*
Mountain Plover, *Charadrius montanus*
Stilt Sandpiper, *Calidris himantopus*

American Bittern, *Botaurus
lentiginosus*
Black-crowned Night-Heron
Nycticorax nycticorax
Ruff (female Reeve), *Philomachus
pugnax*
Long-billed Dowitcher, *Limnodromus
scolopaceus*

6.
All About Distribution:
The Christmas Bird Count.

SOME TIME near the end of December more than thirty-thousand birdwatchers in more than thirteen-hundred local counts will take part in the annual super-ritual sponsored by the National Audubon Society—the Christmas Bird Counts.

If you are at all interested in birding or in birds, even as a new birdwatcher, you will probably be a part of this army of birders. Beginners may be asked to keep the checklist or to count the numbers of a given species, while more experienced watchers make the identifications. But whatever one's degree of expertise, the CBC is a time of good fellowship for all birdwatchers and of friendly competition among groups. It also provides one of the best opportunities of the year to bird with experienced and reliable birders and to add life birds to one's list.

But what is it all about, this counting of birds? Why do so many otherwise sensible people get involved, tramping about outdoors in hard-to-reach places, often in nasty weather? What is so important about getting started before dawn? Why is the continuity of many counts over many years so very important? The answer is distribution.

The total number of species and of individual birds within each species counted is computerized, and these numbers may then easily be compared to numbers reported in past years. In this way we learn, among other things, which species are moving or expanding their ranges, which are proliferating, and which have diminished in numbers to the point of being endangered or even extirpated.

If distribution is so important, why shouldn't the same principles governing CBCs be applied to everyday birdwatching? Indeed, they should be. Every bird walk should be a CBC as far as record-keeping is concerned. Conscientious birders keep daily logs as a regular thing, including species seen, and designating, if possible, the numbers sighted of male and female, adult and immatures of each species.

Learning the distribution of birds will increase your interest in birding and will make you a better birder. To your present joy in watching and in answering the question, "What is that bird?" simply add the query, "Does it belong here *now?*" Ask yourself, if you are not already doing so, such things as: "Where did the bird come from and where is it going?" "Is it early this year?" "Is it staying on longer this winter?" Merely raising such matters creates a state of mind that leads to more accomplished birding.

Keeping accurate checklists or a daily log, with numbers, not only will help you know what to expect when you return to a particular area another time, perhaps years later, but also will enable you to exchange information with other birdwatchers, alerting your community to the local status of birds and to arrivals and departures. Further, such records add to the general store of ornithological knowledge, and as has often been pointed out, there is no other field of science where the amateur can and has added so much.

Because birds are capable of crossing oceans as well as whole continents and are able to come and go across borders without producing passports or visas, there are still gaps in the story of distribution, some glaring gaps (and inasmuch as the story is ever-changing, there always will be). Every birdwatcher should be involved in the effort to refine what is already known and to fill in what we do not yet know.

Learning how far north a bird nests, how far south it winters, and how far east and west it ranges adds romance to the sport of identifying birds. With minor exceptions the range descriptions in the American Ornithologists Union Checklist (Fifth Edition, 1957) are accurate and complete for North American species, and the volume is broken down into subspecies. The recently issued Sixth Edition has been expanded to include Central America, Mexico and the West Indies. This left no room to include subspecies. I am given to understand the ranges in the new edition are not all accurate and should be used only as a general guide. Later revisions will surely correct this and the broader dimensions add a new excitement to what we like to call "our North American species," many of which actually spend much more time below our southern border than they do here.

American Birds, a bimonthly magazine issued by the National Audubon Society, regularly publishes the results of the Winter Bird Census, the Spring Breeding Bird Census, and the Christmas Bird Count (CBC). The regional reports will reveal what is common in your area through the different seasons.

If you sight an uncommon bird at a particular time of year, do communicate that to your regional editor (names and addresses of editors are listed for each region). If the bird is uncommon, rare, or accidental, include a description of the bird with your information. The regional editor will appreciate hearing from you, and although you may not receive personal acknowledgement, you will probably find your sighting in print.

Read as much material as possible dealing with birds or birding in your own county, your state, your region—start in your own backyard and expand from there. If there is no area Audubon chapter or local bird columnist you can ask, again your regional editor will know how and where you may acquire books, field guides, pamphlets, checklists. Study all state, province, county, or parish bird lists you can lay hands on, and always save checklists from every park you visit. Though checklists are perhaps the least reliable of all the above material, they are a starting point.

Find an authority knowledgeable about your area, ideally one who lives nearby. Be very polite and very persistent about setting up a correspondence or a series of chats regarding the status of your region. Ask questions. Don't be timid. Ask, ask, ask—and take notes. There are many ways you may learn more about distribution, but your own awareness is the key.

The failure to understand distribution may lead to misconceptions that can creep into the birding literature. And a misconception in print lingers on for generations. Why? Because the literature itself will influence sightings.

For many years virtually every piece of birding literature stated that the most common Peep on the East Coast, presumably even in winter, was the Semipalmated Sandpiper. Despite the revelation by Allen Phillips in 1975 that wintering *peeps* on the Atlantic coast are quite probably if not assuredly all Western Sandpipers, surprisingly, the Christmas counts from that area each year contain reports of Semipalmated Sandpipers. Birders on the Atlantic coast should be aware that after mid-October by far the dominant *peep* present is the Western and not the Semipalmated Sandpiper, and they should also bear in mind that there is no stigma attached to the "Sandpiper—species?" designation when not absolutely positive of identification.

A knowledge of distribution will also help you to relate your area to the larger whole, which is very important. For example the Gray-cheeked Thrush and the Veery are common migrants in the east. Both winter in South America, and there is virtually no record for either in North America in the winter months. They are, in fact, unknown in Mexico and Central America in winter! A review of the CBCs, however, reveals each year a sprinkling of each. Such records, according to some experts, obviously pertain to the Hermit Thrush. The latest fall record for the Gray-cheeked Thrush is of a bird collected at the Brooklyn Botanic Gardens on December, 16, 1910, according to John Bull's *Birds of the New York Area*. Likewise, the only valid winter record of the Veery known to this author is of a crippled bird at Greenwich Point, Connecticut early in January of 1980.

Freedom of flight precludes iron-clad, nonchanging range border-lines within which a bird species is confined. Factors such as loss of food supply or loss of nesting habitat due to forest depletion, weather changes, extreme fire damage, volcanic action, dam-building, and flooding or other like catastrophes, natural or man-made, can change the population or shift the range of a species dramatically.

Thus, in their range maps the authors of bird books make guesses when indicating the extent of migration patterns and nesting and wintering range limits. Most are educated guesses. Some are wrong. (*The Birds of Canada*, by W.E. Godfrey, because it is concerned with some of the world's great breeding grounds, is excellent; and Roger Tory Peterson's recently published *Field Guide to the Birds East of the Rockies* has exceptionally good range maps.)

If you discover a bird where an author says it is not supposed to be, write him in care of the publisher and tell him so. He will appreciate your information and add it to his stock of data for possible later revisions. This is an area of constant change, and, together, we are, all of us, learning all the time.

After a birdwalk, a good habit to get into is to read up on the status and distribution of birds one has just sighted. Then, if you have spotted a bird that, from the literature or the maps, should not have been where it was at that time of year, you may want to go back out to see the bird again and confirm what you thought you saw before.

What is the significance of this? (1) You may have a rare bird which may be a first for the area or may confirm a previous record. (2) There may be an error in the literature that your observation will help to correct. (And this may be even a slight error; perhaps the bird is not supposed to arrive until September, and you find it in August.)

Whether the funny-looking bird you sighted proves to be a rarity or an unusually early or late sighting, the best method of substantiation is through the birder's awareness of the significance of the sighting. Should he see a Swainson's Thrush in December, for example, but be unaware that said thrush is esentially unknown in winter, he will not really study the bird at all. On the other hand, being so aware, he will take copious notes and write pages of description. Nothing impresses the reviewer of a record more than a birder saying, "I knew the bird didn't belong there; I looked at the graph and saw it didn't belong there."

If it is a rare bird, it is important that you do not immediately merely accept the fact that you are looking at a rarity. Your state of mind should be such that you are trying to talk yourself out of the record sighting. Only in this way will you go through its characters critically, feather by feather, to convince yourself of the true identity.

To be aware of the significance of the sighting of a rare bird, the birder must be fully aware of the distribution of the common birds. The purpose of the CBC—aside from the joy of visiting with old birding friends—is to refine our knowledge of distribution. So the importance of reporting only birds you are sure you have seen should be stressed. One presumes the reason strange sightings show up each year is because the counters are treating the count too casually and/or they are perhaps allowing the spirit of competition to run away with them.

CBC compilers have more than strange sightings through binoculars to contend with, but indeed it has happened that a compiler has biased himself in favor of listing, without too much question, a doubtful species. As a hypothetical example: The Gray Catbird and the Brown Thrasher are common in summer in northern Ohio. They are both found wintering from the southern states on south. At the Christmas count both are reported, say, in small numbers (indeed a few of both species linger over in the northern states), and the compiler accepts them with the explanation that after all, the winter has been a mild one.

Now a Gray-cheeked Thrush is also reported, and if the compiler does not keep distribution records in mind, he may easily rationalize, "Well, if the other two are present, it is not hard to understand the presence of a Gray-cheek." The compiler has biased his decision to accept the record because of the readily acceptable Catbird and Brown Thrasher.

Although regional editors usually catch these problems, all of us should be aware of such anomalies. The eastern expression for a bird that lingers behind in winter, the "half-hardy," does not include the Gray-cheeked Thrush by any accepted authenticated record, except that referred to previously. More detail should be required for a report of that bird in Pennsylvania in winter than, say, for a Varied Thrush or a Townsend's Solitaire, both western birds and both more likely drop-ins in the East in winter.

Indeed, western birds that do make appearances in the East (e.g., the Lark Bunting, the Western Kingbird, the Say's Phoebe and the Sage Thrasher) are all highly migratory. The same is true of eastern birds—which include the many eastern warblers—that show up as rarities ("anticipated rarities") in the West.

On the other hand, it is fairly safe to say that the western resident birds (e.g., the Brown Towhee, the Crissal Thrasher) will never show up in the East. A Brown Towhee seen on the East Coast is misidentified or is out of a cage. The appearance on the opposite coast of a nonmigratory bird heightens suspicion of an escape.

Interestingly, vagrants set patterns over a period of time. To know when a vagrant could pop up makes birding more enjoyable. In the West birders regularly go out looking for the eastern Blackpoll Warbler from mid-September to late October. In the East from mid-September to mid-November birders look for the regularly expected Western Kingbird.

For every bird we observe we should have a concept as to whether it belongs or not. As with all animals, every species of bird has its own niche. We should each become as aware of a misplaced bird as we would of a misplaced piece of furniture in our home. This world is, after all, the home we live in.

7.
A Birding Diary.

April 30, 1976. We are on South Padre Island on the Texas Gulf Coast, and it is raining. It is a torrent of rain. The next morning the newspapers reveal we had eight inches of rain in five hours, five inches of that in forty-five minutes! This is the kind of spring weather front birders pray for hereabouts.

Great clouds of birds migrating north push off from the Yucatan Peninsula to cross the Gulf of Mexico. With no opportunity to rest and to reoil their feathers they must fly nonstop across eight hundred miles of water. A strong weather front makes a perilous journey even more hazardous. With wind-blown rain tearing at them, it is an all but impossible adventure. Hungry, cold, their feathers sodden and heavy with rain, many birds drop to their deaths on the crossing. In total exhaustion, those that make landfall drop onto the first shrub or bit of greenery they chance upon.

Ironically, this most trying stage of the migration provides bird-watchers with a most impressive spectacle. Tantalized by our friend Victor Emanuel's colorful descriptions of it, we have come to experience the event firsthand.

At dawn, the rain over, we are out inspecting the low-growing scrubby growth just back of the beach. And it is covered with bird life, literally covered with birds. On a single large shrub there is so much color—the birds all in mating plumage—it can only be described as a brilliantly decorated Christmas tree...a Christmas tree with live ornaments!

The iridescent blue of the Indigo Buntings, the array of vivid colors set like jewels around the scarlet underside of the Painted Buntings, the deep brown on male and the greenish yellow on female Orchard Orioles, the ripe orange color of the Northern (Baltimore) Orioles, the violet blue of the Blue Grosbeaks, and here and there the crimson-fronted blush of the Rose-breasted Grosbeaks—great gobs of color interspersed with tiny brush strokes of almost every hue in every tint and shade in brown (rufous, chestnut, bay, cinnamon, buff); yellow, red and blue, green and gray, and white and black; the rainbow colors of warblers—all perched to rest, to sleep, to preen, to feed on the same bush!

The birdwatchers are agog. An occasional awestruck gasp is all that penetrates the regular drum roll of the nearby ocean breakers as we try to absorb this mind-boggling scene. We are so close there is really no need for it, yet one observes birders raising binoculars—to confirm what was seen with the naked eye—and quickly lowering them.

The before-breakfast bird list for an hour or so of walking up and down between wet shrubs in the clean-washed air covering an area the size of approximately five city blocks is:

Warblers: two Blue-winged, five Tennessee, fifteen Yellow, ten Magnolia, one Black-throated Green, two Cerulean, three Chestnut-sided, one Bay-breasted, two Blackpoll, two hundred Common Yellowthroats, a single late Yellow-throated, six Black-and-white, one rare MacGillivray's, one Hooded, one Wilson's, two Ovenbirds, twenty Northern Waterthrushes, and eight American Redstarts.

The others: one hundred Northern Orioles, fifteen Orchard Orioles, thirty Indigo and ten Painted Buntings, fifteen Green-backed (Green) Herons, two hundred Gray Catbirds, four Gray-cheeked Thrushes, one Swainson's Thrush, one Yellow-billed Cuckoo and one Black-billed Cuckoo, one Eastern Wood-Pewee, five Blue Grosbeaks, six Rose-breasted Grosbeaks, fifty Eastern Kingbirds, one Western King-bird, two Scissor-tailed Flycatchers, one Dickcissel, five Lincoln's and two Lark Sparrows.

August 14, 1977. We are in Descanso Gardens in La Canada at the northern edge of Los Angeles just below the San Gabriel Mountains. We have decided to bird here today to determine what effect the worst drought this area has experienced in recent times has had on bird life.

Mid-August is a dull time for birding in these parts. Worse yet, the hour is 11:30 A.M., a quiet time for birds, and this being a Sunday many visitors are about. What can be said about birding at the worst possible time at a site so familiar (I had led monthly birdwalks here for more than eleven years!) it is "dog-eared." The Salton Sea after a hurricane it is not.

A pair of House Finches pass in their roller-coaster flight, female after the male, along the neat row of magnolia trees bordering the parking lot. The southern California foothills this time of year are normally one of two colors...dry brown or burnt black. The air is yellow with brilliant sunlight, and it is very, very hot. Because of the drought, water has been completely withheld from the surrounding hills.

Here on the floor of the valley, and as a result of extra watering, the expanse of lawn is lush green, and the camelia, azalea, and rhodo-dendron gardens under the healthy stands of California live oak create a welcome oasis for the avifauna. Beyond the tiny pond inside the entrance, Brewer's Blackbirds—males with white eyes—strut like stately drum majors. It is extraordinary that this all-black bird should have such a grossly conspicuous white eye! Drab by comparison, the female is brown with a dark eye and does not qualify for the role of majorette. We hear a soft chuckled *Heh-heh-heh* from a Mockingbird as it hops into the air, wings raised, tail spread—exactly as Audubon first painted it!—flycatching.

The House Sparrows present—as they are everywhere, it seems—peck about at the edge of the pond finding and eating seeds, insects, bits of popcorn dropped by children, bits of fruit—anything. Like the ubiquitous Starling, the niche this species fills in the society of birds seems to have no limits. They are wonderfully adaptable, and not only in their feeding but in nesting needs as well, taking advantage of the warmth afforded in man-made signal lights in cold weather and of the cool of free-hanging flower pots under patio roofs in hot weather.

A Mourning Dove moves quietly in the shade of a crab apple tree (an imported planting), its dark eyes locating weed seed to pick at, its pointed tail carried sedately just above the ground. Two juvenile Spotted Doves sit in direct sunlight at the top of the same tree, unmoving, unblinking, seemingly doing their utmost to be invisible. Their tails are wide and rounded, as is that of an adult feeding nearby. The obvious age difference is that the adult wears what appears to be a fine lace black and white mantilla over her "shoulders," whereas the youngsters' napes largely lack this rich pattern. So as not to frighten them, they are so delicate in appearance, we walk on, pretending they are indeed invisible.

As we approach a peach tree heavy with ripe fruit, a Brown Towhee silently slips behind the heaviest branches and disappears. A Scrub Jay glides in and perches at the top of the tree so he may better police us. The narrow white supercilium (eyebrow) distinguishes him from other jays. It wears a faded blue "necklace," and turning about, it shows its brown "saddle." It emits a few hoarse screams, then the bill remains wide open—its ventilation system—as it eyes us warily.

We quietly slip up on the Brown Towhee to observe it hopping into the air and scratching with both feet simultaneously at the ground litter. It picks, swallows, then cocks the smooth brown head to assess us with one brown seemingly outraged eye, and swoops off, its buffy crissum (under-tail coverts) showing clearly as the long brown tail disappears in the shrubbery. We wonder how many out-of-staters, without checking the bill shape, have spotted that crissum and mistaken it for the California Thrasher!

From a little bridge just within the border of the live oak forest we watch and listen to the swift stream of water race down the hill between mossy green banks, and in this heat we drink in its coolness gratefully. (The recirculated water is pumped back up the hill.) The gray squirrels, in seemingly perpetual play, flaunt their long plumed tails as they scamper under, over, and through the oak trees.

We pause to inspect where some ten years or so ago there had been a gaping slit in the trunk of an oak that served for several years as a hideaway nesting site for House Wrens. The slit has now, with scar tissue, grown together. Time does heal...leaving House Wrens to find new nesting sites. We hear a chorus of tinkly sounds, then see a flock of tiny acrobats—Bushtits—nervously moving about, now upright, now hanging head down and swinging perilously on the twig trapezes, nibbling at wee insect life in the cool parasol of the sycamore trees.

Ahead of us a covey of California (Valley) Quail crosses the path with dainty little steps; then, startled by our presence, the last few seem to pull up their skirts as they thrust their necks forward and run pellmell into the underbrush. When they no longer sense danger they go about their feeding, scratching and picking much as do chickens, scraping with one foot at a time at the heavy carpet of dead leaves. We have long ago decided the harlequin-faced male is even more beautiful than the Montezuma Quail. When the head darts forward to pick at food, the jet black head plume (actually composed of several feathers)—an inverted comma mounted on spring wire—quivers. The brown and drab female has but a stub of a comma atop her head. The white "stretchmarks" (they only so appear!) on the flanks and belly of both sexes are noteworthy.

Now we are in the "wild area" back of the main pond, beyond the birdwatching station, in a stand of very tall eucalyptus trees where the slightest movement of the air results in a murmured rustle of the long thin leaves. In springtime, in the years we led the walks, we would point out the many hummingbirds here feeding on eucalyptus nectar.

We listen to the popping-corn call of a shy Wrentit from the chaparral-covered hillside and recall the long-ago day when leading a walk here we came upon a mother coyote who, after chasing out of the park two very large dogs that had been harassing her, paused on her way back to her pups to challenge our party from a distance of perhaps thirty feet. When she realized we were merely birdwatchers she just as suddenly turned and calmly trotted up the hill and out of sight, presumably to her lair.

The fern garden stream is yet another lovely place where water laughs aloud in the midst of this drought. Oh, and that blur of a bluish bird that just dived headlong into the rhododendron was obviously a Blue-gray Gnatcatcher.

There is an especially quiet spot on the trail above the Hospitality House, which is at the highest point of the domesticated park area, and we must check there before leaving. We climb the leaf-covered steps high up to the fence and a locked gate. There in the overgrown shrubbery a California Thrasher is feeding. Unlike the towhee it brushes the leaves aside with its cycle-shaped bill. And, like the Brown Towhee, it has a rufous crissum, though darker.

The excited scolding of a wing-flipping Ruby-crowned Kinglet joined by the irritated rasping trill of a hidden Bewick's Wren sends us down the hill and on our way rejoicing.

November 18, 1977. For two weeks there has been talk about the first sighting north of Mexico of an Eared Trogon at Cave Creek Canyon in the Chiricahua Mountains of Arizona. Those of us who have had the opportunity to observe the regular-nesting, coppery-tailed Elegant Trogon in that same area know that seeing this new arrival will indeed be the treat of treats. Not only is the Eared Trogon a first for the North American AOU checklist, but we have it on good authority that even in its "home" in west-central Mexico (Durango-Sinaloa) it is "rare and very difficult to find." Thus, when the phone rings and we are invited to join Shum Suffell and Jim Clements to fly to Cave Creek in Jim's plane, the answer is, "YES!"

Arrangements have been made with the small airport at Douglas, Arizona, for a tie-down of the airplane and a car rental. But because that out-of-the-way airport shuts down at an early hour, dusk finds us high over the frenzied Friday evening Los Angeles traffic, looking down on acres of impatient cars. Being released, by aircraft, from the fixed concrete pathways of urban life is a wondrous feeling!

Almost immediately we are beyond the clutter of the city and over what appears to be a desert fairyland far below. Soon there is almost total darkness, broken from time to time by small clusters of street and house lights below—the big Friday night in a small desert town!— and occasionally by a single house light—"There's a dim one; possibly a lantern!"—and now and then a lighted water reservoir that shines up at us like a shimmering bowl of green jello.

Thanks to a good tail wind we are only two and a half hours getting to Douglas. The plane is tied down—we hope securely enough, in this wind—and after a welcome Mexican dinner in town we drive through the darkness to Cave Creek's South Fork campground. We make our way to an open parking slot and stop there. In the total darkness we each find a spot to throw out our sleeping bags to fit as best we can around and between the sharp boulders generously strewn under a canopy of sycamore trees. The depth of leaves we pile beneath us is tinder dry, crackling at our slightest move, and what we hope will be a soft mattress very soon becomes hard rock.

The wind, which has been constantly increasing in velocity, is in a fury, hurtling through this narrow canyon so that its moaning soon becomes shrieking. We pull the hoods of the sleeping bags over our heads to keep out the avalanche of blowing leaves, but must occasionally peek out to admire the brilliant starry sky through the dancing, swaying branches overhead. We sleep fitfully. We are awakened by the wind wildly shaking the trees over us, and from time to time we must reach out of our bags to clear away what seems an ocean of dead leaves accumulating in a windrow over us, lest we be buried alive. And, too, there are the javelinas (peccaries) that periodically appear out of the darkness to snort and grunt and paw close to one's head. But they are easily scared away.

At dawn the wind has stilled, and after a cold snack we go single-file down into the forested canopy of oak and pine and madrone, following a path along the stream. Very soon, around a curve, down a slight decline, near what is known hereabout as "the pool," we hear a croaking call, and, quickly looking about us, see *two* Eared Trogons, a few feet apart, obviously a male and a female! This is overwhelming. We had never dared hope for more than a single bird.

The male is resplendent, the brilliant vermilion on the belly contrasting with the lush green of the breast and head. It is larger than its Elegant Trogon cousin which breeds here regularly, and the underside of the long dark tail shows a very large white rectangular patch, another difference. It is small-headed, with a rather short blackish bill, and the dark eye has a gray eye ring. And, unlike the Elegant, there is no white band separating the vermilion from the green at the breastline. The feathering of the ear coverts juts out slightly to the rear of the head, which, we surmise, gave it its name. The female is very similar, but paler all over. On her the vermilion is pink and the shiny green is gray-green.

The birds are feeding on the berries of a madrone tree. The madrone they are in is a massive old tree just beyond the stream bank, wide-spreading and low-hanging. The bark is copper-colored, like manzanita; the berry fruits are red and grow in clusters out of clumps of long shiny green leaves.

We are all eyes and ears, as hushed as is the forest, for several long minutes. Suddenly the male bird flies off up the trail and into the tangle of trees, cackling loudly. The female follows shortly. The spell is broken. We let out a whoop of sheer joy! We had anticipated a long hunt, possibly most of the day. Had we found only the male we would have been well satisfied. After but a short jaunt we have had excellent looks at both the male and female! Our good luck is...well, almost unbelievable.

By noon we have returned the car and stand ready for take-off. The wind, however, is by this time again gusting in great torrents. Should we chance it? Should we wait? We take off. That wind might howl on for four straight days. Jim's expertise gets the plane off the ground, nose into the wind, and at perhaps fifty feet elevation we seem to be stationary, that is, soaring but not moving forward. Like a California Condor we are aloft, but without its "fingertip" maneuverability. The engines roar, and slowly, inch by inch, it seems, we rise, and finally, not unlike a condor, we seem to find a thermal that carries us out of what for a very long time appears to me to be a heroic confrontation with a tornado, and we are moving ahead.

We fight the wind all the way back to Santa Monica Airport, but there is no feeling of peril; the trip gives us some insight into what routinely some birds endure. And not even a tornado could still the excited chatter of three avid birders who have just seen a pair of Eared Trogons!

BIRD LOG

NOTE: *The following birds were spotted by Mr. Bernstein on the birding trip(s) described in this chapter. They are in the order they were sighted.*

SOUTH PADRE ISLAND, TEXAS:
Indigo Bunting, *Passerina cyanea*
Painted Bunting, *Passerina ciris*
Orchard Oriole, *Icterus spurius*
Northern Oriole, (Baltimore race), *Icterus galbula*
Blue Grosbeak, *Guiraca caerulea*
Rose-breasted Grosbeak, *Pheucticus ludovicianus*
Blue-winged Warbler, *Vermivora pinus*
Tennessee Warbler, *Vermivora peregrina*
Yellow Warbler, *Dendroica petechia*
Magnolia Warbler, *Dendroica magnolia*
Black-throated Green Warbler, *Dendroica virens*
Cerulean Warbler, *Dendroica cerulea*
Chestnut-sided Warbler, *Dendroica pensylvanica*
Bay-breasted Warbler, *Dendroica castanea*
Blackpoll Warbler, *Dendroica striata*
Common Yellowthroat, *Geothylpis trichas*
Yellow-throated Warbler, *Dendroica dominica*
Black-and-white Warbler, *Mniotilta varia*
MacGillivray's Warbler, *Oporornis tolmiei*
Hooded Warbler, *Wilsonia citrina*
Wilson's Warbler, *Wilsonia pusilla*
Ovenbird, *Seiurus aurocapillus*
Northern Waterthrush, *Seiurus noveboracensis*
American Redstart, *Setophaga ruticilla*
Green-backed Heron, *Butorides striatus*
Gray Catbird, *Dumetella carolinensis*
Gray-cheeked Thrush, *Catharus minimus*
Swainson's Thrush, *Catharus ustulatus*
Yellow-billed Cuckoo, *Coccyzus americanus*
Black-billed Cuckoo, *Coccyzus erythropthalmus*
Eastern Wood-Pewee, *Contopus virens*
Eastern Kingbird, *Tyrannus tyrannus*
Western Kingbird, *Tyrannus verticalis*

Scissor-tailed Flycatcher, *Tyrannus forficatus*
Dickcissel, *Spiza americana*
Lincoln Sparrow, *Melospiza lincolnii*
Lark Sparrow, *Chondestes grammacus*

DESCANSO GARDENS, LA CANADA, CALIFORNIA:
House Finch, *Carpodacus mexicanus*
Brewer's Blackbird, *Euphagus cyanocephalus*
Northern Mockingbird, *Mimus polyglottos*
House Sparrow, *Passer domesticus*
Mourning Dove, *Zenaida macroura*
Spotted Dove, *Streptopelia chinensis*
Brown Towhee, *Pipilo fuscus*
Scrub Jay, *Aphelocoma coerulescens*
Bushtit, *Psaltriparus minimus*
California Quail, *Callipepla californica*
Wrentit, *Chamaea fasciata*
Blue-gray Gnatcatcher, *Polioptila caerulea*
California Thrasher, *Toxostoma redivivum*
Ruby-crowned Kinglet, *Regulus calendula*
Bewick's Wren, *Thryomanes bewickii*

CAVE CREEK CANYON, CHIRICAHUA MOUNTAINS, ARIZONA
Eared Trogan, *Euptilotis neoxenus*

8.
Migration:
Long and Prolonged.

WHEN SPRING COMES for most icebound and winter-worn birdwatchers that means Migration (with a capital M). The mere mention of that single word "Migration," a highly romantic word, is enough to start the old wellsprings flowing again.

Because most birdwatchers think of the migration only as the arrival or passing through of springtime warblers, for them it simply does not begin to happen until March. The seductively colorful warblers have indeed cornered the market on spring migration, and inasmuch as the same birds are dull, drab, and "confusing" in fall plumage, the spring migration is the only migration many birders care to even participate in. There is, of course, much more to it than that.

Actually the migration of birds goes on virtually all through the year. In the East as well as the West the spring migration first becomes evident in late February when the swans, ducks, some gulls and some geese—in the main fully adult and urged on by the desire to breed—leave the wintering grounds and move north. Because other gulls, ducks, geese from south of you are filling the gaps in the over-wintering flocks, the early departures may be so subtle you may not even miss those leaving.

The flocks that migrate this early will go to open lakes, slowly feeling their way north, until they reach and find their breeding grounds hospitable. Immediately they will commence mating and nesting. (Much of the pairing, especially among ducks and geese often has already taken place before they arrive in the land where there is "daylight all night.")

This scenario commences in February, and it is not uncommon to see geese still flying south in December! One can easily see that this narrows the time during which there is no evident migration at all to near zero.

In the West by mid-January Allen's Hummingbirds have arrived, and by late January Northern Rough-winged Swallows join them on the coastal slopes of southern California. In the heart of the country, say in eastern Iowa, the Roughwings do not arrive until April, of course, and the Ruby-throated Hummingbird will not make an appearance until May.

Spring melts its way north, it is said, at a pace of fifteen miles per day. Naturally, the seed-eaters (sparrows, finches, grosbeaks, etc.) come first. They are followed in a few weeks by the insect-eaters (vireos, warblers and lastly by the flycatchers). Feeding requirements necessitate that most songbirds and shorebirds migrate at night so they may feed during daylight.

Of course, soaring birds, the raptors, Wood Storks, White Pelicans and often gulls migrate only during daylight, as the first two depend on upwelling thermals and the last feeds on the wing, as do the swifts. Waders and swimmers that feed in day or night migrate either in day or night, according to our Fish & Wildlife Service, and diving ducks are prone to migrate over water at night and over land by day.

Spring migration is indeed an extended process. Such diverse birds as the Empidonax Flycatchers, Blackpoll Warblers and White-rumped Sandpipers are still moving north in mid-June, by which time the first Wilson's Phalaropes are on their way south, followed at the end of June and in early July, by the first adult shorebirds. Remember, adult shorebirds do not accompany their young south. The juveniles come on later. And this is in fact true of the passerine populations, although they cover a much broader front and there is some overlap, of course.

With the passerines, and again very broadly, the farther north the breeding grounds the later they leave their wintering havens, and thus the later they come through your neighborhood. Why? Because if those that nest in the northern boreal forest were to leave wintering grounds too early they would arrive in blizzard conditions.

Thus it is that Kentucky and Hooded Warblers, birds that need not move far north but nest in our southern states, arrive on the Texas coast in late March, while the Blackpoll, Cape May, Bay-breasted and Chestnut-sided Warblers that nest much farther north come through in May, late in the spring migration. Obviously this leapfrog pattern evolved so those nesting in the far north will not arrive there in April, when they would either freeze or starve to death.

The juveniles among the passerines make their appearance headed south in the fall looking for the most part like their mothers—but, in fall plumage, so do most of the fathers.

Although I am leery of such "guesstimates," fall migration, when an estimated twenty-billion birds, adult and young, move south, is, for the songbirds and the shorebirds, much more strung out than is the spring mass movement. Certain urgencies are not present in the fall, and young eyes are seeing the world about them for the first time, so there is more of a tendency to drop in and feed for an extra few days here and there en route south.

There are fewer birds, of course, to go north in the spring. It is again "guesstimated" that only 10 percent of the birds born any spring will be alive to return the following spring. I have also heard that perhaps only a third return. Take your pick. It is obvious there are fewer birds moving north in the spring than there are going the other direction in the fall.

It has been said that before calling a shorebird you should know its age. Indeed, learning to age shorebirds will make a better birder of you. Juveniles born in June do not reach adult plumage until August of the following year when they molt into winter plumage. Being aware of their age and distribution, and knowing that the adults leave for the south often weeks earlier than the newly-hatched young, helps in determining whether the bird is to be expected or is a very rare bird at a particular time.

The fact is that adult shorebirds leave their young at about the time the natal down has changed into juvenile plumage. The next possibility of a chance meeting between them would be on the wintering grounds, to which the young find their way without assistance, although here again there is some overlap.

There has been some confusion between Semipalmated and Western Sandpipers on the East Coast in winter. Because it is related to migration and is an interesting story, it deserves to be told.

At a time when virtually every piece of birding literature referred to the Semipalmated Sandpiper as being "the most common Peep in the East," presumably even in winter, Allan R. Phillips did an investigation which included examining Semipalmated skins in every museum of any size in the country. His remarkable findings were published in the August 1975 issue of *American Birds*.

It was determined that with but one single exception every Semipalmated taken in winter on the East Coast was actually a Western Sandpiper. The single exception had been taken at the southern tip of Florida. Some of the bird skins had been misidentified and mislabeled for years.

Distinguishing between these two in the field is, in all fairness, no easy matter. Generally among shorebirds the female has a comparatively longer bill than the male. And because there is overlap in the sizes of bills as between female Semipalms and male Westerns there has been some confusion in identification.

It is now believed that in July and August adult Semipalmated Sandpipers on leaving the north fly directly down through the eastern half of the country to their wintering grounds in the Caribbean. In the West the great majority of fall records are of juveniles.

While the migration path of the Semipalms is being further investigated, those seen in the East from late August to early October are almost all newly feathered juveniles. By October the juvies have gone through and it is presumed those Semis reported in the East on the Christmas Bird Counts are Western Sandpipers, which cross the country in small to moderate numbers to winter in the East. And inasmuch as they all molt into winter plumage on arrival, the juvies would be difficult indeed to pick out from the adults among them.

With reference to other shorebirds, the first to come south through California, for example, are worn looking. They are the older birds who look ready for a dry-cleaning job. They are still in alternate (breeding) plumage and some have started their postnuptial molt, but it is only as they arrive on or near their wintering grounds (for some species far to the south) that they will get their full new set of winter feathering.

So it is, on both coasts, that by late June the majority of the adult population of shorebirds has passed through. There is variance, however, as to the arrival dates on the opposite coasts. Migration is later on the East Coast, most noticeable in the juvies. For many species the juveniles arrive on the West Coast by late July, while on the East Coast not until mid-August.

This variation is due, perhaps, to the colder continental climate affecting the tundra in middle and eastern North America so that the nesting cycle starts later than in much of Alaska where spring comes earlier. As a general rule, on their winter grounds before migrating north, shorebirds undergo a pre-alternate molt, so as they move north they are in breeding dress.

All through the lower forty-eight states, even in the middle of the country, from mid-August through September shorebirds moving south are mostly juveniles and can be identified as such because each feather is fresh and unworn and their upper parts mirror the adult in breeding plumage. Unfortunately, most field guides either do not show the juvenile shorebirds or they are mistakenly mismarked as adults.

The Baird's, Pectoral and Buff-breasted Sandpipers seen on both coasts during fall (late August to mid-October) are juveniles, the adults having gone through earlier. But it is, of course, not so simple. Baird's Sandpipers migrate north through the mid-portion of the country in the spring. In fall the adults come back south through the middle of the country and the juvies follow, but some juveniles move south along the East or West Coast.

The migration pattern for the Buff-breasted Sandpiper is the same except that some juveniles return south along the East Coast—with some straying as far to the east as the British Isles—and a few moving south along the West Coast. It is ironic that this American species is more numerous in Great Britain than it is on our own West Coast.

Pectoral Sandpipers move north in springtime in a broad front through the East and Midwest and return in fall along, generally, the same routes. It is a scarce bird in the West except in fall when small to moderate numbers are seen from late August to late October, all are juveniles and obviously migrate south on a broader front than do the adults.

We witness vertical migration principally in the West where there are a substantial number of mountains reaching high altitudes. There is a tendency, unfortunately, to overemphasize the extent of this type of migration. Some birders have assumed that the wintering Dark-eyed Juncos, Purple Finches, American Robins and in some years Golden-crowned Kinglets and Red-breasted Nuthatches have come down from the local mountains, whereas most, if not all, have come from localities much farther north. Obviously, paying attention to the subspecies involved could help unravel where the birds come from.

Nevertheless, because a few feet of altitude is equivalent to miles of latitude, vertical migration is in regular usage in the West by such as Mountain Chickadees, Western Bluebirds and Anna's Humming-birds. The Anna's is common on many valley floors in the far West through the spring and early summer, when many disappear. They have deserted the valleys for the cooler mountains nearby. Then, each December, again because of weather, they move back down to the valleys where we find them feeding on the nectar of winter-blooming eucalyptus trees, the wide assortment of exotic imported yard plantings, and the insects they attract.

Aside from the regularly anticipated small numbers of "disoriented vagrants" from the East, it may come as a revelation to at least a few birdwatchers that some species commonly thought of as eastern breed not merely north but also west, some along the Pacific Northwest and Alaska. The American Redstart, Blackpoll Warbler and Red-eyed Vireo are examples.

It is apparent that each spring a goodly number of so-called eastern species make their way actually northwest, either by flying diagonally across the continent, or, as does much of the Bobolink population, by traveling up the east side of the Great Plains and then due west to summer and nest across the entire upper half of the Upper States. There is a reversal of these courses in the fall.

Inevitably there is each fall a small movement of these so-called eastern birds south through the Pacific states and interior Southwest. It has been said that the Southern California fall warbler list includes more "vagrant" species than "regular" species. Many of these birds by abandoning the ancestral flyways are merely going south for the winter. Of the unknown number of birds that take this coastal route some actually make it, meeting up in Mexico or Central America. A good percentage of these migrants do not make it, particularly those oriented in a southwesterly direction; they meet their demise over the Pacific Ocean. This, of course, occurs more or less in reverse during spring migration, but not to the same extent as in the fall.

A true lateral, or at least semilateral, migration seems to occur in the case of the Little Gull which moves from northeast to southwest and back again to breed on the steppes of Russia and to winter off the coast of Spain.

In our own West we have the "Silky-Flycatcher Caper" which is strangely different, if not unique, among North American species. Each year the Phainopeplas inhabit the lower deserts, such as the Colorado and Mohave, from late September through April. After a first nesting the vast majority fly over to settle on the coastal slopes— to nest again! Presumably this satisfies feeding requirements.

This spring try to write in your personal logbook the date that each species makes an appearance in your area. Highlight that date with a red pen so you can easily pick it out. Do the same again in the fall for the last time you see a departing species. By the next year you will have something to compare these dates with and you will have a much better familiarity with your birds. You will also enjoy the fringe benefits of thinking back on a notation, reliving the place and the time, the friends you shared it with, the sounds, the smells and the excitement of the complete experience.

9.
Be Prepared:
The Salton Sea in Summer.

WHEN YOU PREPARE to bird an area new to you, be sure to familiarize yourself—as much as possible—ahead of time with any hazards you may encounter. And beware—trips to a particular area in the winter months may be of little or no help at all in summertime. Often it is a different place!

If there are descriptive writings dealing with the Salton Sea in summer season I have not come across them. An experience there in my early birding days should act as a caution light to those who anticipate visiting this birding hotspot in summertime.

It was like something one would find only in a dream—a bad one. A chain of crises occurred comparable only to the oldtime matinee thrillers that reached a climax every Saturday with the heroine tied to the railroad tracks while an out-of-control engine bore down on her. Perhaps it was only a dream.

The story really starts out on a Friday night following a "rare but regular" nightmarish work week as a court reporter and I had to "get away." The pleasant voice of the nice lady on the Los Angeles rare bird alert (at that time Jean Brandt) said, "There are Fulvous Tree Ducks (now called Fulvous Whistling-Ducks), Wood Storks, Black Skimmers, Gull-billed Terns, and a Lesser Golden-Plover at Salton

Sea." To the pleasant-voiced nice lady goes the credit for what followed—and secretly some of the blame for it, too. After all, isn't there something in the law about presenting an attractive nuisance?

I didn't know the Salton Sea, and I certainly did not know it in summer. I had been to that sink—and at two hundred thirty-five feet below sea level, it is just that for runoff irrigation water, including its salts, from the vast surrounding farmlands of the Coachella and Imperial Valleys—only twice before, on organized, well-conducted winter field trips, when birdwatchers make the trip if only to gaze in wonder at the comings and goings of the tens of thousands of Snow Geese. I had never been to the north end. That is why I wrote out Guy McCaskie's instructions so carefully—and unfortunately left them next to the kitchen telephone when I left home at 3:00 in the morning.

The sun is coming up rosy red as I enter the mini-town of Mecca, where I do recall I am supposed to look for the dike leading to the sea's north end. But as I turn right off Highway 111 I think of Jim Lane's advice to look for Crissal Thrashers in the fields of mesquite out of Mecca, and so I am diverted into chasing that bird until well scratched up and satisfied; by 7:00 A.M. I must have been four miles beyond the Lincoln Avenue dike, which is what I should have been looking for. But at this point, without my written directions, I am not aware of that. And, after all, a dike is a dike, and one could take you to the sea as well as any of the others.

A hard left takes me up onto what appears to be a solidly compacted dirt dike. Then, perhaps a half mile toward the sea, I come upon a sapling laid across the top of the dike. Strange. I get out of the car and remove it—and see what some farmer was trying to warn me of, a washout—actually a good foot of nothing, a gap, in the middle of the dike.

There is barely room for one car to ride atop the dike, certainly not enough room to turn around in. I could, of course, back up the half mile or so, but how, then, would I ever reach the north end of the sea and the Black Skimmers there? Cha-a-a-r-g-e!

I back up enough to give myself a good running start, then floor the Magic Red Maverick and sprinting forward, hurdle the gap. Not an original trick; I had seen it done in a movie. I stop on the other side, get out and pull the sapling back across the road to warn other motorists, and then go on.

I high-hurdle two more washouts before it dawns on me I am on the wrong road and must retreat. How to turn around? Ay, there's the rub. Surely I would never be able to negotiate four miles or so of rutted and bumpy single-lane dike-top in reverse. And there are the washouts to think of!

Following a flock of Savannah Sparrows, the little, yellowish faces now glinting in the sunlight, I take a down ramp into what appears to be a dry stream bed. Down I go. Then forward—oh, oh! There is a direct relationship between the depth your rear wheels have sunk to and the sensation expressed by, "I could feel my stomach drop."

Outside the car I discover this is not really sand, it is a fine silt. The rear wheels of the vehicle are up to the hubcaps in gray flour! There is not a house anywhere I can see, nor a person, nor a telephone pole or electric line. Now there is not even a Savannah Sparrow. I am completely alone in unspoiled nature.

I take my binoculars, look back once to wave perhaps a permanent goodbye to my faithful automobile, and trudge my way toward the highway. About three miles back, in jubilation, I hear the welcome sounds of heavy machinery. Cutting across a field or two and carefully slipping through two barbed-wire fences, I locate a farmer working a tractor in an orange grove. He finds it hilarious that I am here to look for birds.

He does accept the challenge and is waiting at the car with his tractor when I finally reach there. By 10:00 A.M., the car is pulled back up onto the dike, headed back, for a very nominal five dollars.

As if in a movie, now I see myself driving slowly out to the highway, and I see the farmer standing on his tractor shaking his head in disbelief when I get out to remove the first sapling roadblock. I make my way back out to the road and then retrace my path toward Mecca and, on the good advice of the farmer, to Lincoln Avenue and the proper dike. From where Highway 111 comes into Mecca a tobacco chewer could easily spit to the right and create a puddle on Lincoln Avenue.

It is but a short distance on that dike to the north end of the sea. And here, at long last, is my first life bird of the day. Near the shoreline a Black Skimmer neatly unzippers the flat water surface with its lower mandible.

I watch two of the big birds for a while, then realize the sun is high. I can feel its heat, and so I head south on 111 for a stop at Red Hill

Marina. It is after 11:00. Looking for the reported Wood Storks, I first come upon a mud flat where, with three Black-bellied Plovers, feeds a Lesser Golden-Plover. The amber coloring on the back is strikingly apparent.

Locating the Wood Storks is no problem—they are large and obvious—and there are perhaps fifty birds in the flock of largely immature post-breeding wanderers. They perch in dead low trees or stand on the ground in the sun cleaning and preening themselves. Thus I log my second and third life birds of the day. And out on the beach area there is the fourth, a Gull-billed Tern—many Gull-billed Terns flying about, foraging along the edge of the sea. Only one more bird, the Fulvous Whistling-Duck, to go!

The sun is straight overhead now, and as soon as I start the car engine I turn on the air-conditioner. God bless this man-made environmental improvement! I am headed around to the headquarters area when I fortuitously come upon a tiny neighborhood grocery store. I quickly purchase a quart of some cold soft drink, open it, and, sitting in the shade outside the store, raise the bottle and drink the quart. Oh, how refreshing! I had, of course, very stupidly started out on this venture with no water at all, without even a thermos of coffee. Beeeg mistake!

Lugging my scope, I am walking up the path in the headquarters area. The sun is glaring. Everything around me is tinged with yellow. I feel as if I am in an oven. The sun is incredible now, and I can feel the heat rising from the hard-baked white bleached earth.

Overhead and all around me are raucous, screaming Black-necked Stilts, not merely protesting my presence in their nesting grounds but attacking me, singly and in pairs, while shrieking what must be the worst bird language epithets ever heard. A few American Avocets are also present, adding to the ruckus. I actually hold my scope and tripod at the ready to fend off a diving bird that does not veer away at the last moment. The noise is deafening.

I am sure it will cease when I reach the edge of the south end of the sea beyond the HQ building, but it continues, constant and unremitting. A thermometer on the outside of the building reads 112°F. The air is close and filled with the noxious odors of decaying matter mixed with the hot stench of the sea. A half hour of trying to look for ducks while ducking looks of hatred from the stilts under these conditions has got to qualify an infantryman for the Bronze Star.

I stagger back to the car and to the cool air and make straight for the same wee grocery store and its red icebox. I snatch up a quart of the cold drink, snap off the cap, and uptilt the bottle. When I am finished I turn to pay the wizened little Mexican proprietor with the skin of polished mahogany. "Wha' you doin' here?" I explain about the five life birds I seek. His daughter interprets, and they both laugh. Then he speaks, and the daughter says, "He say the sun will cook your brain."

But I am already thinking about how to capture my fifth life bird of the day. Wading up the New River at the south end of the sea would be all but impossible in this heat and stench. I race out to Highway 111 and head north, then turn east on a dirt road. At 3:00 P.M. I am at Ramer Lake. The ranger just leaving tells me it must 118° out here. Dainty Ground-Doves feed around the ranger station.

It is a small lake, and I can bird the entire way around it from the air-conditioned car. There are hordes of Red-winged and Yellow-headed Blackbirds and many Snowy and Cattle Egrets, but I must concentrate on the Fulvous Whistling-Duck, and there are none—not until dusk, when they start coming in from feeding in the surrounding fields to settle securely in Ramer Lake for the night feeding session. I shut off my car engine while I walk about studying my fifth life bird of the day. Another beeeeg mistake.

Returning, I discover the car engine will not start again. Running the air-conditioner, often while the car was at a standstill, may have drained the battery. So, I can always sleep in the car until the ranger returns on Sunday—or will he?

With typical birder's luck I discover one other car parked not far away, and its owner is glad—no, I would say anxious—to get me started with a set of cables. Very soon I am roaring up Highway 111 toward civilization.

According to my records, all this occurred in 1972 in either July or August. I can't tell for sure because the month is smeared—probably from sweat—and illegible. (I now know it was August because the Savannah Sparrows arrive at the sea by late July.) Or was it only a bad dream—with a happy ending? After all, I did see five life birds!

BIRD LOG

NOTE: *The following birds were spotted by Mr. Bernstein on the birding trip(s) described in this chapter. They are in the order they were sighted.*

MECCA, CALIFORNIA:
Crissal Thrasher, *Toxostoma dorsale*

SALTON SEA, CALIFORNIA:
Savannah Sparrow, *Passerculus sandwichensis*
Black Skimmer, *Rynchops niger*
Black-bellied Plover, *Pluvialis squatarola*
Lesser Golden-Plover, *Pluvialis dominica*
Wood Stork, *Mycteria americana*
Gull-billed Tern, *Sterna nilotica*
Black-necked Stilt, *Himantopus mexicanus*
American Avocet, *Recurvirostra americana*
Common Ground-Dove, *Columbina passerina*
Red-winged Blackbird, *Agelaius phoeniceus*
Yellow-headed Blackbird, *Xanthocephalus xanthocephalus*
Snowy Egret, *Egretta Thula*
Cattle Egret, *Bubulcus ibis*
Fulvous Whistling-Duck, *Dendrocygna bicolor*

10.
"Bird" as a Second Language.

THE COMPLETE birdwatcher recognizes each bird species by the sounds it makes. This is, obviously, of inestimable value in bird identification.

Caw-caw! says the crow. Easy to recognize and to remember. You immediately determine on hearing it that an American Crow is in the vicinity. "Bird" is many languages, and some of the other nine thousand or so avian cries and whispers abroad in the world may not be so easy. That is the challenge. But look at it this way: If a bird wanted to learn the five thousand or so languages of man recognized on this planet, that would be even more of a challenge.

Each spring I am overcome with the feeling of *déjà vu* as I listen once again to the warbler sounds. And despite many years of birding and listening, all too many birds sound to my still uneducated ear as if they were speaking in tongues. I am happy to know I need not cope with translation. All I am faced with is the relatively simple task of distinguishing between a robin and Red-eyed Vireo, much as I have learned to recognize French from Russian. It is almost the same thing. There are chips and calls, and there are songs. Indeed, there are also hoots and quacks and honks and whistles, but space will limit my discussion for the most part to passerines.

87

You already know, I am sure, that most of the common, contented chipping we hear, both spring and fall, is a means by which birds stay in contact. In "Bird" the maxim is: "The flock that chips together stays together." A wee bird clambering about in a hopeless tangle of shrub and vine would, without sound effects, be all alone very quickly and thus be deprived of all the goodies the flock is discovering as it moves cloudlike through the woods.

When it seems otherwise quiet, the alert birdwatcher will follow the call of the chickadee, inasmuch as this bird is usually at home in the territory others are merely passing through and so knows the best food sources, and also because it calls loudly and often, and frequently will be found leading a mixed flock of warblers. It goes without saying that skulkers (i.e., Connecticut and Mourning Warblers) prefer to go it alone and are only rarely found in such a flock.

For some birds there are flight calls, as opposed to the same bird's normal chip, and there are panic calls, feeding calls, and usually a "let's-keep-the-flock-together" call. Listen for the flight call either just as the bird propels itself into the air or while the bird is in flight, so that it is "rained down" on the birdwatchers below. Horned Larks—well, all larks—are famous for this, and their song is high-pitched and light and beautiful.

But then again, a flight of some thirty-thousand Canada and Snow Geese has rained down on me such a deafening cacophony of quack, cackle, and gabble it is almost frightening. And although from where I stood, looking up, I could not tell, I suspect most of it—well, half for sure—was from the females. While many male ducks, if heard at all, merely whistle or *kwek* to keep in touch, it appears the females *quack* loudly and seem to gossip nonstop.

Every true birdwatcher knows the real opera season commences not in the fall but in the spring. For this is bird opera, and the sound of bird song can be as lyrical and delightful as anything coming from the stage of the Metropolitan.

Human singers of renown have taken on such names as "Southern Thrush" or "Irish Nightingale"—bird names—but even the Carusos and Pavarottis were never called upon to sing solo, a capella, loud and clear, with "pear-shaped tones" after being perched all night in a heavy rainstorm or, body scrunched down, feathers fluffed up, through a below-zero night, desperately trying to keep the young from freezing. That would have been demanding even of John McCormack, and there is probably a union rule prohibiting it.

Many of the songs in the fall are not what they were when mating and nesting were in progress in springtime. Song in the fall is often shortened, being rendered commonly by the young birds practicing. Also, individual birds will produce in fall a song different from that sung in spring. Although the eastern Rufous-sided Towhee admonishes *Drink your tea-ea-ea*, I have heard the resident Song Sparrow in our West Virginia yard sing *Drink your tea-ea-ea, laced with cinnamon*, all through the spring, and the same bird by late August had changed its song to *Tee-hee-hee-hee...Gotcha!*

There is also in some species a noticeable change in pitch which should be listened for, usually from very high in the young bird to a deeper sound in the adult. A good example of this is the high-pitched squeal of the young Caspian Tern, which changes with aging (unlike a good whisky mellowing) to the familiar raucous squawk.

Then there is song dialect. Dr. Luis Baptiste of Occidental College in California, who has done extensive work on the subject, demonstrated long ago that the common race of White-crowned Sparrows wintering in southern California, *gambelli*, sounds different from the race of White-crowns resident in coastal and central California, *nutalli*. There exists, in fact, neighborhood differentiation. And certainly when we get into the mimics, such as mockingbirds and thrashers, if you have been listening you are aware of wide variation. The mockingbirds in Marietta, Ohio, do not imitate Scrub Jays and Hooded Orioles, for example, as do the mockers in Malibu, California. Each, obviously, copies the sounds of its own environment. There is also individual variation in the same species, the same race, the same neighborhood.

And if by now the recognition of "Bird" sounds impossible or very difficult, it really is not. It is certainly no different from recognizing two Frenchmen in conversation. Naturally their voices are not exactly alike, nor do they mouth the words in precisely the same way, but you know they are both speaking French and not Greek or Russian or Spanish. In learning "Bird" all you are asked is to identify the speakers as Frenchmen, Germans, Brown Thrashers, or Yellow-billed Cuckoos.

There are the generally accepted, standard methods of learning.

The National Audubon Society has marketed a gadget which plays the song of the bird whose picture is inserted, and this may be very helpful. The National Geographic Society recently made available an album covering songs and calls of some two hundred otherwise difficult to identify North American species. The Cornell University Laboratory of Ornithology puts out bird songs on tapes, as well as phonograph records designed to play, species by species, the calls and songs of the birds in Roger Tory Peterson's eastern and western field guides. One of these may be your thing. Peterson himself, in his recently revised eastern field guide, however, points out that "in learning bird voices (and some birders do ninety percent of their field work by ear) there is no substitute for the actual sounds."

The best way I know of to learn chips, calls, and songs is to run down each bird, one by one, in the field, and thus couple the sound with the live bird. And, again, take notes while doing so.

The books in trying to describe bird song to the reader tend to break it into syllables. This helps. The translation, however, from "Bird" to English I have consistently found surprising, occasionally astonishing, and almost always, to me, amusing. The birdwatcher, you see, can only translate "Bird" into something in English from his or her own background. How a particular bird song is interpreted, in fact, may reveal the part of the country where the interpreter was reared.

To a midwesterner the California (Valley) Quail says. *Chicago! Chicago!* To a westerner close to the Mexican border it says, *Chicano! Chicano!* Furthermore, to a freight dispatcher or a ship's bosun it says, *Check cargo! Check cargo!* The eastern Rufous-sided Towhee's *Drink your tea-ea-ea* to a criminal attorney sounds like *Cop a plea-ea-ea*; a lumberman will hear *Cut a tree-ee-ee*: and the pet shop owner hears *Scratch a flea-ea-ea!*

Obviously the suggested words, sounds, or phrases in any field guide are meant only as just that, a suggestion of the sound, a syllabic count you can perhaps remember and refer to, even if you do change the wording to make it more your own. Also, of course, there are some bird calls that defy being bent into English words. Take, for example, the steamboat whistle calls of the Yellow-headed Blackbird, which are described as "low rasping sounds" in two of the field guides.

Very few of the suggested phrases in the field guides may match what you hear, but most of them will be close. Peterson says the

Rose-breasted Grosbeak goes *Ick* or *Eek*. To many it says, *Peek!* I hear more *Piddle-dee, piddle-dee, piddle-dee* from the Carolina Wren than I do the more popular *Tea-kettle, tea-kettle, tea-kettle*, though I have heard them both.

And like any good beer drinker, I prefer *Quick, three beers!* to *Check, three beers!* from the Olive-sided Flycatcher. It's a toss-up whether the Blue Jay says *Kick it! Kick it!* or *Bridgit! Bridgit!* and I suppose this would depend on whether one ever knew a lovely girl named Bridgit. I do go along with *Pick up the beer check, quick!* in preference to *Chick-a-poreea-chick!* for the White-eyed Vireo.

I offer the following chirping gratis, not that the birds will say the same things to you they say to me, but merely as a starting place. Some are the same as, or similar to, what appear in the books, but you may adopt or modify any that appeal to you. Here are some warblers interpreted by birders across the country:

Chestnut-sided: *Very, very pleased to meeeet you!* Hooded: *To meet, to meet, to meet with you!* Kentucky: *Churie, churie, churie!* (or *Cherry*). Common Yellow-throat: *Witchity, witchity, witchity!* Ovenbird: *Teacher, teacher, teacher!* Cerulean: *One, two, three, SNEEZE!* Prairie: *Zee-zee-zee-zee!* (up the scale). Blue-winged: *Bee-z-z-z!* Golden-winged: *Beeeee-z-z-z!* Yellow: Sweet-sweet-sweet-so very sweet! But the Yellow-throated: *Sweet-sweet-sweet-sweet-sweet!* (down the scale). Black-throated Green: *Zoo-zee-zoo-zoo-zee!*

The Red-breasted Nuthatch sounds like a tin horn and the Acadian Flycatcher like a bathtub duck but also like one of my favorites: *Pizza!* Yellow-throated Vireo: *Elsie, Elsie, come here!* or *Helen* or *Vera*, etc., and the Ash-throated Flycatcher, *Ka-brick!* The White-throated Sparrow says *Old Sam Peabody!* The Red-throated Pipit gives a high-pitched *Speeeze!* The Red-eyed Vireo: *Here am I. Where you are?* The American Redstart answers very rapidly: *See-see-see me in the tree!* The Summer Tanager mutters *Sit down. Sit down.* The American Goldfinch says *Potato chip!* or *Chip-chip-chickory!* The Indigo Bunting talks in paired notes. *Squeak-squeak! Squeak-squeak!* and then *Spit!* The Lapland, Smith's and McCown's Longspurs all give a similar dry-rattled *K-r-r-u-m-p!* or *P-r-r-t!*, but only the Chestnut-collared Longspur calls *Kiddle-diddle!*

To some the Worm-eating Warbler sounds like a sewing machine, and the Yellow-breasted Chat, the archetypal suede-shoed salesman with the "gift of gab," is referred to by some eastern birders as "ole garbage mouth" because it yammers so in "Bird" jargon. The Great crested Flycatcher says *Wheeeep!* The thrushes are, of course, flautists practicing their instrument in the woods, and the Brown-headed Cowbird has a high thin whistle and calls me by name, *Chuck!*

Toward the end of a long and tiring day of birding the sounds do indeed take on new meanings. At such times I have heard the Tufted Titmouse sing *Martini! Martini! Martini!* And on an empty stomach, with the sun disappearing the west, I have heard clearly the Barred Owl's *Who cooks for you?* which reminds me of the Yellowhammer, a British bunting that accusingly snarls, *Little bit o' bread and no cheeeeese!*

Tom Heindel a birder from east of the Sierras, tells of walking through the woods on a long-ago trip to Mexico when the exceptionally quiet afternoon was shattered by a very loud, very human burst of laughter. *Ha-ha-ha-ha-ha-ha-ha-ha!* It was contagious: he and the two with him started to laugh, wondering what was so comical. They moved toward the laughter and were amazed to find the source in a nearby tree! It was a Laughing Falcon, buff underneath with a dark brown back and face mask. The three birders cracked up and laughed all the way back to their motel. Remembering, he still bursts out in laughter.

Mitch, Tom's son, has embarked on a project he thinks will take the "confusion" out of fall warblers. He is taping chips and calls of all warblers, both in the East and the West, so that by listening to them they may be compared in hopes one may more easily learn to distinguish between them. He hopes to tape every North American warbler, so this may take a while.

An article in the May 1981 issue of *American Birds* deals with a quiet but persistent controversy that has been raging around a bird call. Tim Manolis, a California birder and obviously a proven birding literature detective, unravels in almost comical fashion the history of the "kicker" song. Overly-simplified and in brief: A particular song in a marsh was tentatively attributed by one ornithologist in 1901 to the Black Rail; but in 1902 another ornithologist heard a similar song from a Yellow Rail, captive in his kitchen! Over the years it has been attributed, always by different ornithologists, to Virginia Rail, then Clapper Rail, and finally King Rail; and the description of the call went from *kick-kik-kik-ki-queeal* to *tic-tic-tic McGreer* to *kek (-kek-kek)-burr* to *kek (-kek-kek)-hurrah* to *kik-kik (-kik)-kurr*, even *kip-hip-hurrah*, and even the foreign *tjick-tjick-tjick-tjuirr* of the Eurasian Water Rail! And although Tim, the super-sleuth, has unraveled the story, with a fine sense of humor, the mystery still remains.

The value of learning to link bird identity with chip or call or song is, of course, undeniable. So go on out into the field, and learn it, the hard way, but the fun way.

11.

Of Shorebirds and People and Condors.

I CAN HEAR her yet. "Quinny, call out that White-eyed Vireo I hear."

Bz-bz, squeak-squeak-squeak!

"There he is, right in front of Quinny, in the left side of the tree."

"Amazing!"

"Not really. Have you ever seen a catbird?"

"No. No catbirds in California."

"Oh, we'll fix that. Quinny, squeak Chuck out a catbird!"

Quinton, the speaker's husband, a short, thin, amiable man, his baggy trousers flapping around his ankles, shambled over to the side of the road, bent over slightly, staring into the heavy thicket, and, by sucking at the base of the extended index and middle fingers of one hand, produced a catlike squall that almost immediately brought out a catbird.

My wife, Elsie, and I were captivated. It was sheer magic.

We had been birdwatching for several years, but this was our first birding in the East, and our first trip to Cape May, New Jersey, and we had the good luck, in a parking lot, to meet up with Evelyn and Quinny Kramer, from Philadelphia. She was bright, generous with her vast knowledge, bubbling with birding enthusiasm, and knew, it seemed, where every single bird was hidden on Cape May. She and

Quinny showed us our first Solitary Sandpiper, and when she learned I'd never seen a Bobolink they drove us to a nearby field of, I think, oats and told me to just run through it. I did and brought up an immense flock of Bobolinks.

She was very kind to a pair of not exactly mere beginners—but we weren't at that time into "serious" birding, either. It will never be said of me that I hide under a bushel my joy at seeing a "good" bird. And she shrieked with pleasure at my expressive reactions to each life bird produced. Birding with them was an enchanting experience. It was also contagious.

Evie mentioned, when we parted, that there had earlier been seen a Buff-breasted Sandpiper on a sand spit nearby. Following her directions we crawled through a fence and found the spit but weren't really sure, having never seen one before, what we were looking for.

We wondered whether it would look like the picture in the book, or was it one of those birds with differing color phases, seasonal variations or what I thought of then as "growing pains" (pains to the birdwatcher) because of size and color differences from the pictures we found in the field guide? So when Elsie quietly said, "Look what landed behind you; bet it's a Buff-breasted Sandpiper," I think I jumped a little. It was buffy all right, down to the belly.

Two elderly gentlemen were in conversation at the end of the spit and obviously waiting for the bird to make its appearance. I yelled to them, "Are you looking for this bird?" It was feeding at the edge of the water perhaps twenty feet from where Elsie and I stood.

One of the men deigned to turn and look our way; the other didn't bother. We just knew they knew—they were positive—that with their years of field experience they'd find the Buff-breasted if anyone did; it would be a put-down to have it pointed out.

The man who'd looked our way then slowly raised his binoculars as if expecting to come up with a House Sparrow, stared a long time, uttered something that turned his companion around, and then they were both staring through their binoculars at what is one of North America's most exciting shorebirds. But they acted very, very cool. An everyday occurence, y'know, I heard one mutter. "Of course. Anybody who couldn't recognize a Buff-breasted would have to be blind!"

Elsie and I studied the bird for a few minutes and left. It was to be twelve years before I would see the next one.

𝒥

After only a few weeks in our West Virginia hideaway close by the Ohio River I begin to pine for my California mountains and their birds, my deserts and their bird life, and most of all my Pacific Ocean, its gulls, its pelagics and especially its shorebirds. With time the yearning can only be compared to a hunger. By fall, aside from Killdeer, I am starved for the sight of a shorebird.

The year 1981 is no different in that respect. On a birding day on September 2, I remember the Hebron National Fish Hatchery and head on I-70 toward Columbus, Ohio. The time of our first birding in the East, September 16, 1969, marked the time of my last visit, when Elsie and I had seen Baird's Sandpipers in the mud of an emptied fish pond and had witnessed excitement and delight when Elsie's mother, the late Maude Bunner, saw (at age eighty-four!) a bird through a spotting scope for the first time—a Great Blue Heron. How sad to have waited eighty-four years before really looking at a bird.

Over two hundred acres in size, the hatchery is made up of a series of earthen basins (filled with water from nearby Buckeye Lake via the old Ohio Canal) where fish are hatched and at the proper age and size distributed to the lakes and streams across Ohio. There is also an extensive marsh area attractive to rails. For many years, indeed until his recent retirement, it was supervised and watched over by Fritz Griffith, a man who (luckily) is as devoted to birds as he is to fish. Migrating shorebirds stop over to feed in the rich sediment of the drained ponds.

Aware that one birdwatcher (who knows the territory) is worth a thousand birds, I am delighted to find Gina Buckey scoping a pond from outside the fence. The information she passes on to me is most exciting. She had been informed that both Stilt and Buff-breasted Sandpipers were recently seen in the drained ponds. If we could find them they would be life birds for her.

Though the basins are not wall-to-wall with shorebirds, there is some action out there, and the possibility of those two "good" birds still being present has me lit up like a fistful of Fourth of July sparklers in the hand of a kid. Gina and I join forces. We are soon inside the hatchery scoping the pond she had been looking at through the chain-link fence—only now she is looking north, away from the sun, which can add definition to the color of a bird.

The zebralike Killdeer are everywhere. A Greater Yellowlegs, another, then a Lesser Yellowlegs beside yet another Greater Yellowlegs. Shorebirds at last! Ah, a rather large bird whose brown breast ends abruptly and evenly at a white belly—a Pectoral Sandpiper, one, two, three of them. Dark gray back covered with fine white spotting—a Solitary Sandpiper, and another. Then a small brownish Peep with a straight bill, heavy at the base and almost bulbous at the tip, picking, picking in the mud—a juvenile Semipalmated Sandpiper.

"This could be the bird!" I focus in on a bird smaller than a nearby Killdeer, about the size of a Solitary. It has a soft, smooth "feel." It is a plump, long-winged bird with a rather long neck in comparison to other small waders and a cap of fine dark streaking; each black feather on the back is edged in silver, and buff covers its cheeks, throat, neck, and breast down the front. The flanks are buffy white, belly and undertail coverts almost pure white.

Moving slowly on yellowish legs covered with layers of gray-green muck, it disappears behind the merest hump in the otherwise flat basin bottom and reappears soon, picking its food with a delicate, thin, straight bill that, like its bright eyes (accentuated by a thin white eye ring), is black in color. Seeing the flash of white underwing when it "stretches," we exclaim aloud. Gina has one life bird—a Buff-breasted Sandpiper!

Concentrating now on the neighboring basin, we comb out a Semipalmated Plover, three Least Sandpipers, more Solitary and Pectoral Sandpipers, and finally the Stilt Sandpiper. It is a rather large bird with a back more gray than brown over brown primaries. The underparts are a dirty white. It has a white eye stripe and a dark cheek patch and a rather long, black bill—stout at the base and narrowing and down-turned at the tip—that probes deep in the muck for its food. This bird hops on one long leg and drags the other, perhaps injured on its journey from northern Canada to Mexico or even South America.

Two life birds for Gina! She is almost as excited as I am. I feel I am reveling in shorebirds, and it is only with great reluctance that I move my scope away from one to seek out another. Two other birders make an appearance to view the birds; one is Fritz Griffith, who had first found the birds and alerted Gina to their presence; the other is his long-time birding friend, just a few days before his eighty-second birthday, he tells me, the still vigorous Dr. Milton B. Trautman, who had come down to see the birds.

It takes no time at all to find the birds again, and following a most welcome conversation (about birds, of course), I am left alone in the gathering dusk, my scope still scooping in shorebirds, my thoughts going back to my first Buff-breasted Sandpiper twelve years before.

♫

In the east the sky is covered over by a gray, lumpy cloud-cover quilt, the underside lit with pink and coral and gold. It is 6:30 on this chill morning in 1981, and though it is December 9, there is no snow, no ice—there is not even rain. In this valley called the San Fernando, the leaves of the parkway liquidambar trees, some scarlet, some yellow, fall lazily in silence, as would feathers out of an opened pillow. Intermingled with the shower of leaves, also in silence, a flock of Dark-eyed (Oregon) Juncos drops down, a few birds at a time, wary and uncertain, tilting and teetering slowly, so that from a distance it is all but impossible to distinguish between birds and leaves. Leaf color is the only indication of the season.

Hal Ferris, my birding buddy, makes his appearance, and we're off, targeted for Mt. Pinos, the Edmonston Pumping Plant just beyond, or possibly "the new place," on our annual pursuit of the California Condor.

I saw my first condor on August 16, 1966, at the Sespe condor refuge up the hill from Fillmore. I've seen many since then. On one field trip I led a caravan of cars into the parking lot just below the top of Pinos. As we exited the cars preparing for the short hike to the top, an adult condor soared over, perhaps fifty feet above the parking lot. I yelled, "Condor overhead!" The group viewed the huge bird, ooh'd and ah'd, and ten minutes later when I gathered my "field-trippers" together I was startled to learn only a handful remained. They'd seen what they had come to see, had re-entered their cars, and started back down the mountain!

The montane species I pointed out to the remaining few—even the Green-tailed Towhees scrounging picnickers' crumbs around our feet—were mere anticlimax. For a field trip leader it is better not to find the condor until late afternoon! I counsel "Pinos pilgrims" to wait for Audubon condor warden John Borneman's famous "four o'clock condor," which has occasionally accommodated eager bird-watchers right on time from the 8,831-foot mountain.

In late fall at the Edmonston Pumping Plant, just east of Grapevine, one looks for soaring condors over the ridges to the south and combs the hillside live oak trees for roosting birds. But August is prime time for finding this endangered species in its sanctuary, inasmuch as August 8 each year is the start of deer hunting season, and the entrails left on the mountain wherever a deer is taken are an additional lure—this still being calving season—to the stillborn calves and dead cattle that attracts this carrion eater. Today we hope to prove from a "new" lookout at the back of the mountain and much lower down that it is possible to view this big bird almost any time of the year, and that the chance of seeing it is much better than from any of the other three well-known viewing sites.

At eight o'clock, just north of the San Fernando Valley on State Highway 5, we identify from the car five Tundra (Whistling) Swans on Pyramid Lake. By 8:30 we are sipping hot coffee in a small cafe just off the Frazier Park exit, the turnoff for Mt. Pinos. We also clean our binoculars, careful to first moisten the lenses, and make our plans. We will bird our way to the top of Pinos and investigate the "new" condor hotspot on our way back down, for one must give the sun time to create the thermals on which condors move.

Hal and I bird our way up the mountain, and when we arrive at the intersection with Mil Potrero we stop to examine the wide patch of thorny impenetrable scrub. For a few minutes we walk about quietly and hear only the wind. Bird silence is in force. Then we hear chips. An LBJ (little brown job) flies out of one clump of brush and dives into another to the right. Suddenly there is another LBJ zooming to the left, and before we can get our bins on them, two more fleeing to the right, and instantly disappearing!

(I have become cognizant of clever, unanticipated diversionary tactics that can only be a conspiracy, a bird conspiracy. To protect each other, just as you get your glasses focused on a good bird, some other little twit, and always a much more common bird, will cross your field of vision pulling your eyes to the left or right so the desired bird can make a clean getaway!)

Ah, the narrow streaking down the breast, pale eye rings, dark tail with white outer tail feathers—Vesper Sparrow! Gotcha! And now we are in the midst of chinking Dark-eyed (Oregon) Juncos, appearing, scrambling and sputtering like radio static, and disappearing around us all at the same time. Across this high desert foothill Hal and I walk different routes, but I nudge him to "Watch out for Mountain Quail." They could indeed be down here with deep snow near the mountaintop.

I catch a glimpse of the gray and white head pattern of a Sage Sparrow. The wind continues to blow, the chill is piercing and the birds are skulking. Nothing moves. I try my Screech Owl call. Suddenly a brave bird hops atop one of the shrubs—a colorful male finch. But Purple or Cassin's? The brown nape proves it is a Cassin's, and as he flies off two females leave with him.

There is a sharp chattering deep in the thorny shrub. Patiently we wait and watch and are finally rewarded by the appearance of a Plain Titmouse seeking shelter from the wind. We tramp the surrounding fields several times before leaving, adding White-crowned and Golden-crowned Sparrows.

We are up in the pines now—Jeffry, Coulter and ponderosa—and the wind roars like a beginner practicing the tuba. McGill's Campground yields several White-breasted and a flock of Pygmy Nuthatches. We spot a Brown Creeper probing its way along the cracks in the bark of a ponderosa pine. Then, surprise—possibly the birds of the day—a flock of eight Golden-crowned Kinglets! All appear to be yellow-crowned females except for one male which sports a red and yellow crown.

Strange, we have seen no White-headed Woodpeckers; no woodpeckers of any kind! We avoid the high snow drifts but our boots sink into several inches of snow nevertheless. The sky has taken on a flat gray "I'm-gonna-snow-soon" look. I remind Hal of the many Varied Thrushes I saw here just three weeks ago and he perks up and his pace quickens. Is there anything more boring than a bored birdwatcher on a no-bird birdwalk? If your birding buddy gets that "uninterested" look on his face because no new birds have presented themselves for twenty minutes, he is spoiled rotten, as is mine.

Now we are at the parking lot near the top of Mt. Pinos. A quick walk over icy snow through wind-whipped Iris Meadow evokes the feeling that we are moving through a once treasure-filled mansion now abandoned and empty. The wind increases its velocity and frigidity, and wails its desolation.

I remember the many summer days here when, instead of snow, the fields were wall-to-wall green, and lavender iris provided a feasting table for the many tiny Calliope Hummingbirds....The snow crunches underfoot as I make my way to the leaning tree in which a Goshawk perched one summer day....I study the tangle of twisted snow-covered trees and shrubs searching for my Winter Wren of some summers ago....The parking lot itself is forlorn where one summer long ago a California Condor floated low overhead just as a caravan of birders arrived....I can still hear the screams of surprise and delight.

A locked gate bars the way to the top. The devious boulder-strewn dirt road is buried in deep snow. The sky is threatening. We decide hiking to the top would be unproductive.

On our way back down the mountain, I catch sight peripherally of a bird that swoops into a pine tree, a blur of orange and black. I slam on the brakes and point out for Hal his first Varied Thrush of the year. He is astounded by the brightness of color. It is a male bird in clean unworn plumage, each feather perfect. Hal is elated. So am I. It is indeed as exciting to show someone a good bird as it is to see one myself.

On down, down the hill and a left turn at the sign to the left side of the road that reads "Los Padres National Forest" and lists some forty "organizational camps" nearby. It is marked also "Mil Potrero Highway."

(In the summer of perhaps '77, long after Quinny's untimely death, Evie Kramer passed through California, and we briefly birded together on Mt. Pinos before she joined the tour she was co-leading. At this intersection of Mil Potrero we caught sight of something interesting on the hillside to the left of the roadway: quail, with head plumes half worn away, but the wide vertical striping on the flanks clearly identifying them. "Oh, Mountain Quail!" she gasped. She was as excited and as enthusiastic as if it were a new bird for her!)

It is a good two-lane roadway that winds through a small mountain community replete with pond and golf course that I recall looking down on from the top of Mt. Pinos. From this intersection it is 20.1 miles to a turnout on the right side of the road that overlooks to the northeast a good part of the San Joaquin Valley. We can look across miles of farm fields beyond even the Tehachapi Mountain Range, it seems, to the snow-capped High Sierras! This is the "new" place to look for California Condors—and other birds, especially raptors. Behind us to the southwest is Mt. Abel, and behind that, Mt. Pinos.

The scope is immediately set up and we follow two Red-tailed Hawks riding on the wind. Relative size and our distance from each bird now becomes relevant, for we are looking across a stretch of many miles. It is vaguely reminiscent of Hawk Mountain in Pennsylvania. Birding is fast-paced; some bird makes an appearance every few seconds, coming in from behind the mountain or appearing suddenly above the horizon or just below it.

Here are two Prairie Falcons, long wings sharply pointed and very light in color, zooming like shooting stars across the stage and vanishing. Here is a bird chasing another. The chaser is a Red-tailed Hawk, yet compared to the size of the bird it is chasing it is the size of a robin! The chasee? A long cylindrical black body suspended from a flat, wide, long—long!—span of wings, black but for the merest bit of whitish in the wing linings, only finger feathers moving to control its direction—a young California Condor! There is no mistake. We take turns following it in the scope. With the sun on it, the head is a pinkish-gold.

It soars across the highway back of us and is lost behind the hill. As we jump up and down in celebration, for neither of us has previously seen a condor in winter, here it is again, and this time quite close to us there is another condor! The newcomer is also a subadult with whitish flecking coming into the leading edge of the underwing. They circle, and one leaves; then both are gone. Breathtaking!

Directly across from us now soars a white-bodied buteo, its head also very light in color. It has dark leggings, and when it turns there is the cinnamon tail-top—a Ferruginous Hawk! From our left comes a flock of forty Band-tailed Pigeons. Avoiding the wind, they fly just below the crest of the hill we are standing upon. They cross the highway to our right and are out of sight.

"Off to the left!" A Golden Eagle being chased by what may be the same Red-tailed Hawk that chased the condor! Perfect timing for size comparison! We quickly scribble notes. The second chasee is only twice the size of the chaser. The first chase involved a chasee more than twice the size of the chaser. This points up the size difference between the condor and the eagle. We are delighted with our success at the "new spot."

On our way down, and still at an altitude of six thousand feet, our car flushes two birds from the right side of the road. They fly clumsily across the highway and for a short distance alongside the car. Dark olive-blue backs, white "stretchmarks" along the side of the belly, head plumes—Mountain Quail!

And I hear again the delight in that remembered voice, "Oh, of course, Mountain Quail!" and again the bubbling enthusiasm, "Quinny, squeak Chuck out a catbird!"

BIRD LOG

NOTE: *The following birds were spotted by Mr. Bernstein on the birding trip(s) described in this chapter. They are in the order they were sighted.*

CAPE MAY, NEW JERSEY:
White-eyed Vireo, *Vireo griseus*
Gray Catbird, *Dumetella carolinensis*
Solitary Sandpiper, *Tringa solitaria*
Bobolink, *Dolichonyx oryzivorus*
Buff-breasted Sandpiper, *Trygnites subruficollis*

HEBRON NATIONAL FISH HATCHERY, HEBRON, OHIO:
Killdeer, *Charadrius vociferus*
Greater Yellowlegs, *Tringa melanoleuca*
Lesser Yellowlegs, *Tringa flavipes*
Pectoral Sandpiper, *Calidris melanotos*
Solitary Sandpiper, *Tringa solitaria*
Semipalmated Sandpiper, *Calidris pusillus*
Buff-breasted Sandpiper, *Tryngites subruficollis*
Semipalmated Plover, *Charadrius semipalmatus*
Least Sandpiper, *Calidris minutilla*
Stilt Sandpiper, *Calidris himantopus*

SAN FERNANDO VALLEY, CALIFORNIA:
Dark-eyed Junco (Oregon race), *Junco hyemalis oreganus*

PYRAMID LAKE, CALIFORNIA
Tundra Swan, formerly called Whistling Swan, *Cygnus columbianus*

MOUNT PINOS, CALIFORNIA:
Cassin's Finch, *Carpodacus cassinii*
Plain Titmouse, *Parus inornatus*
Vesper Sparrow, *Pooecetes gramineus*
Dark-eyed (Oregon) Junco, *Junco hyemalis oreganus*
Sage Sparrow, *Amphispiza belli*
White-crowned Sparrow, *Zonotrichia leucophrys*
Golden-crowned Sparrow, *Zonotrichia atricapilla*
White-breasted Nuthatch, *Sitta carolinensis*
Pygmy Nuthatch, *Sitta Pygmaea*
Brown Creeper, *Certhia americana*
Golden-crowned Kinglet, *Regulus satrapa*
Varied Thrush, *Ixoreus naevius*

MIL POTRERO CONDOR OVERLOOK, CALIFORNIA:
Red-tailed Hawk, *Buteo jamicensis*
Prairie Falcon, *Falco mexicanus*
California Condor, *Gymnogyps californianus*
Ferruginous Hawk, *Buteo regalis*
Band-tailed Pigeon, *Columba fasciata*
Golden Eagle, *Aguila chrysaetos*
Mountain Quail, *Oreortyx pictus*

12.
Merry Christmas Bird Count.

WHAT COLOR are its legs?" (Imagine! She wants to know the color of its legs!)

I rolled my eyes up into my head for my wife Elsie's benefit. But Elsie covertly shook her fist at me and said, "We'll find out, Clara. C'mon, Chuck!"

We ran back to where our small group kept watch over the sparrow of mysterious identity. Three birdwatchers, not much more experienced (or inexperienced) than we were, looked at us inquiringly.

Out of breath, I whispered, "She wants to know the color of its legs."

One said, "Red," another, "Black"; the third said nothing.

At this point we all looked at the bird carefully for the first time, at least at its legs. We agreed they were pink or flesh-colored. Elsie said, "Go back and tell Clara."

I realized then I was to be the messenger. I ran back to where Clara Weedmark, a retired school teacher then perhaps in her seventies who had a huge store of knowledge about birds, sat in the back seat of a car. "The legs are pink," I gasped.

"That narrows it down. Is it very tiny? Does it have stripes over the head? Is there any white in the tail?" (Oh what the devil!)

"It's a good-sized bird." "I don't think so, but maybe." "Oh, the tail—I don't know." Back I went, hoping the bird had not by now been scared off.

"Is it thick-billed? Is it a seed-eater? Is it scratching at the ground with its feet?"

This is a story of long ago. We had joined the San Fernando Valley Audubon Society, and those good people convinced Elsie—and she convinced me—that we should help on their annual Christmas Bird Count (whatever that was!). They needed all the eyes they could muster, she pleaded, no matter that we didn't know many species of birds. I decided my twenty-twenty vision, aided by a pair of cheap binoculars I had brought home from Germany in World War II, might contribute something to the count, if only in numbers.

Unfortunately, that cold harsh morning the leader of our party did not feel up to walking the grounds of the Olive View Medical Center in Sylmar, California. She didn't look well at all. Secretly we wondered if by the end of the day she might not end up inside the hospital, the grounds of which we were birding. But Clara was a fighter and would not submit to "pampering" herself. Scheduled to lead this section of the count—as she had for many years—nothing could keep her from it. Her history in birdwatching and conservation in California went way back. She and her good friend Helen Pratt had much to do with laying the groundwork for the passage of California legislation protective of wild birds, for the establishment of the Audubon Society in southern California, and for the Southwest Bird Club, purported to be the oldest still-functioning birdwatching organization in the West.

"It's scratching at the leaves on the ground and it has a pretty thick bill!" I was exhausted. Her usually serious face softened with the twinkling of her eyes, then she broke into a warm smile. "Many dark streaks down its breast?"

"Oh, yes!"

"Good. Fox Sparrow!" And she went on. "Now let's review the marks."

I did not, of course, go running back and forth finding the answers to questions all of that long day. By the end of my first Christmas Bird Count—and this is the story of my very first one—the five in our party when we looked at a bird saw it well, at least I did; and I was hooked on birdwatching. And though I have participated in at least one Christmas Count—and often several—each year ever since, I have never again experienced a more unique bird count, where the leader nursed a headache and led a squad of birdwatchers from the back seat of a car! As for Clara Weedmark, she was a great birdwatcher and—a superb teacher.

♫

A hundred miles north of Los Angeles I shiver in the chill morning air and watch the sun creep up on the Antelope Valley. It is December 19, 1981. This, the Lancaster CBC, is my most recent. I am with Jon Dunn, Bruce Broadbrooks, and Hank Brodkin, three heavy artillery pieces of the Los Angeles Audubon Society's birding battalion. Some highlights:

A Northern Harrier high over a field has the dihedral of a turkey vulture, but it does not rock from side to side, nor is a turkey vulture expected to be found here in winter....A House Wren utters a churlish chutter, and I think of the lovely warble it sings in springtime (and I realize that warblers don't warble; House, Winter, and Carolina Wrens and Purple Finches and American Goldfinches, they warble!) and here it is hiding in a shrub near the gate of a farmhouse at the side of the road....Six hundred Water Pipits pass overhead and set down in a nearby field. We do a quick study, for we must hurry to cover the vast high-desert irrigated farmland area we have been assigned....*Chicago! Chicago!* A California Quail. NO! What? A starling, yes, a starling imitating a California Quail!....And here is the one he imitates, the real California Quail!...There. A Merlin *(Falco columbarius)* perched on a telephone pole crossbar. Jon explains we should watch also in this area for the subspecies *richardsonii*: although less often found here, it is paler and would have bright white tail banding....Sign on a gate: "Trespassers will be eaten!" I hear no growl. I peek over the gate. In we go....We have confronted many barking and a few snarling dogs today, but in cooperation with the previously announced and widely publicized Christmas Count this dog is now barking from inside the house (for which we are grateful)....

At noon we meet for lunch and an updating (i.e., what is still missing that we should have already found? Who should look particularly for what, where?) A hawk, blue-gray on the top of it, flies into a tree almost overhead. Several holler. "Cooper's!" Then the correction and the official word from Kimball Garrett and Jon Dunn: "Sharp-shin. Cooper's has a comparatively much longer tail!"...The list of our still-wanted species is read out. We still need a longspur, a Ross' Goose that had been overwintering at the sewage ponds. Mountain Plover, Ladder-backed Woodpecker, Golden Eagle, Rough-legged Hawk—and a Sprague's Pipit would be just dandy.

Now, here, Lark Sparrow, a Roadrunner, then a Vesper Sparrow. ...The to-be-expected afternoon wind is blowing now....Two Myrtles among two hundred Audubon's Warblers....Dark-eyed Juncos—a slate-colored—foraging in a barnyard with Oregons. ...Black and Say's Phoebes....Lincoln's Sparrows in the dry scrub looking much like Song Sparrows—but Song Sparrows without water nearby would be unlikely....Hurriedly we hike across fields covered wall-to-wall with sheep droppings, perusing the twelve hundred Horned Larks, chasing after them, back and forth, back and forth, looking for longspurs. We find no longspurs....Now, a Ferruginous Hawk, showing the white underside of its spread tail....Then, "Golden Eagle overhead!" And so low...beeeutiful!. ...We are now in the cut-over barley fields where this past fall five Sprague's Pipits had been discovered. We walk the fields from side to side, listening, watching intently, combing through hundreds of Horned Larks and Water Pipits. Bruce waves Jon and me back to their field. He found one. Hank is "babysitting" it. Very soon four of us are focused on a Sprague's Pipit that peers back at us mouselike from behind a leaf on the ground. When it flushes it flies perhaps thirty feet or so and then (normal for a rock but not a bird) drops straight down onto the ground again and scurries off to hide in what remains of the already harvested alfalfa....A bird flushes from the brush-filled ditch. "Sage Thrasher!" Good bird. We'd wondered if we would find one for the count...."Overhead, Pine Siskins!"....

To the south we can see snow on Baldy and the other mountains in the San Gabriels...."Ahhh, Prairie Falcon!" I am allowed thirty seconds to study it. Very light buff bird, closely streaked down the front, narrow sideburns. "Let's go!"...Brewer's Blackbirds and Brown-headed Cowbirds feed around the dainty hooves and even on the backs of the woolly gray sheep, reminiscent of the Ox-peckers that so intrigued me in East Africa years ago....Thirty Long-billed Curlews in flight.

On to the golf course and to "Fred's Slough"....We find a Red-breasted Sapsucker and a Red-shouldered Hawk on the golf course. ...When we come out to the road we meet up with other birding parties and get the news that Donna Dittman and Starr Saphire found a Pectoral Sandpiper at the sewage ponds. This would possibly be the third credible record for California in winter!...

Our tour is over. We covered over eighty miles by car. No one mentions the miles we have walked. It is 5:00 P.M. The sun is already very low in the west, and the high desert chill sets in. We have a hundred-mile drive back home. We are tired, dirty, and fulfilled.

🪶

I find great adventure, great romance, in birdwatching, and on several different levels. Often I am awed—no—overawed by these types of common everyday "little" things:

Looking at a Harris' Sparrow in southern California in winter, knowing the bird was hatched last spring in stunted black spruce on tundra edge, perhaps near Churchill, Manitoba....Watching a Baird's Sandpiper in the Ohio Valley's clinging heat of August or September, knowing the bird comes from nesting grounds on Canadian Islands well northeast of Point Barrow, Alaska....The almost constant coming and going of the birds; always the long and mysterious journey, concealed in darkness, veiled in fog, in thunderstorm and hurricane and blizzard....The where-have-they-been and where-are-they-going; the where-will-they-be-next-winter and how-many-will-be-alive-to-return-next-spring?...

I feel astonishment and delight, too, knowing that during the time of one particular Christmas Bird Count birdwatchers, wearing shorts and T-shirts, do their work in sweltering heat while at the very same time another party far off, buttoned-up over the ears, seeks its birds by plowing along on snow shoes in below-zero weather.

Once, not too long ago, men would gather to determine, by how many dead birds they piled up, which team had the best marksmen. Trying to stop this practice, in 1900 Frank M. Chapman organized with twenty-seven birdwatchers the first CBC. Men came with binoculars instead of firearms. Now sponsored by the National Audubon Society, Chapman's new "game" was an immediate success.

Early on, the statistics were published in *Bird-Lore*, the magazine of the early Audubon Societies. The compilation now is printed up each year in the July edition of *American Birds*. I find this issue handy not merely for catching up on the whereabouts of long-unseen birding friends (I always seek out the names of birdwatchers I have known) but also as a source of great fun—I speculate on how difficult or how laid-back it was for a particular birding party to find the birds they did tote up, what hazards they may have encountered, what perils they steered clear of in different parts of the country in totally different climates and conditions.

One should try to keep in mind that this is not merely a competition among friendly birdwatching teams; it is also the annual clash of weather fronts, of changing tides and ocean upwellings and cliff-warmed updrafts, of raging storms far out at sea, and pelting rain and howling winds and snowstorms on land; and these events play a large part in the final totals of each CBC.

For me at least these reports are packed with human as well as avian drama, and if read with but a wee touch of imagination reveal the entire gamut of high adventure, of pathos, of mystery, comedy, glory victorious (and glory less than victorious). From the July Christmas count issue of *American Birds* in just a few different years here is what I mean:

In Pittsburg, New Hampshire, at freezing temperatures of 31° to 23° on December 23, 1977, Davis Finch and Elisabeth Phinney (just the two of them) spent sixteen hours covering one-hundred twenty-eight miles, most by car, in a snow cover of fifteen to eighteen inches, to find, aside from all the usual winter birds of the northeast, two Northern Goshawks, White-winged Crossbills, and twenty-eight Ruffed Grouse.

Just ten days later that same year, in their count circle, which includes a piece of the Pacific coastline as well as some of the Santa Monica Mountains, seventy-nine observers assigned to their stations by Kimball Garrett and Jean Brandt on the Malibu, California count, in temperatures hovering around 65°, put together a most interesting and disparate bag ranging from Black-vented (Manx) Shearwater to California Quail and Virginia Rail!

Also in 1977, in the middle of the country, co-compilers George Griffith and Milton Trautman deployed their fifty observers at Buckeye Lake, Ohio, to tally almost twelve thousand individual birds of eighty-one species in mild winter temperatures, oddly similar to those at Malibu!

On the same day fifty-two observers traveled a total of five hundred twelve party miles (fifteen by boat, ten by airboat, and four by canoe!) in West Palm Beach, Florida, to count their Limpkins, Purple Galli-nules, an array of parrots and many species of warblers. And again on the same day in 1977 in Jackson Hole, Wyoming, in moderate snow at temps of from 7° to 26° (c-o-o-o-l-d!), thirty-nine observers covered two hundred twelve party miles (forty-two miles on skiis and six miles on snowshoes!) to find among other goodies thirty-six Trum-peter Swans, thirty-five Bald Eagles and five species of owls!

Contrast that with the three observers at St. George, Utah, who that year hiked for seventeen miles over their riverbottom/desert count circle in just-above freezing temperatures to tote up thirty-six Gambel's Quail, some Abert's Towhees, and almost a thousand Water Pipits! And that same year, between 8:15 A.M. and 4:00 P.M. in intermittent light rain, fourteen birders (hot toddies at hand, no doubt) aboard the *Kaleetan* ferry between Anacortes, Washington, and Sidney, British Columbia, among other species, counted nearly six hundred fifty Arctic Loons.

In 1970, on the last day of the year, in Park County, Montana, eight observers braved a four-hour blizzard to total ninety-five miles (fifteen on foot, seventy-six by car and four miles—over a period of two hours—on horseback!), ending that long day with thirty-four species, including goodly numbers of Common and Barrow's Goldeneyes, Pinyon Jays, and two hundred forty-five Bohemian Waxwings (which must have made it all worthwhile).

December 16, 1972, dawned on a twenty-four inch snow cover in Fairbanks, Alaska, the temperature during the day dropping from 1° to 7° below zero with a northeast wind blowing at from twenty-two to forty miles per hour. That did not deter the Fairbanks Bird Club. Twenty-seven observers scurried about by car, on foot, and on skiis, and a few hardies counted at their feeders (and who can blame them?) to find ten Willow and three Rock Ptarmigans, among other nice birds; and sad to say, present during the count period but not on count day (I can taste the bitterness!) a Gyrfalcon.

Six days later another CBC took place aboard the *Blue Nose* ferry between Bar Harbor, Maine, and Yarmouth, Nova Scotia, during which six observers spent six hours in temperatures from 14° to 20° (one can just feel the tears running down cheeks!) in what is described as a "fairly calm sea with some swell," producing some life birds for southern Californians Jerry and Laurette Maisel and sufficient material for George Plimpton (an observer of the observers) to write a somewhat comical but barbed articled detailing that count and later published by *Audubon Magazine*.

Also in 1972 ten observers in Sackville, New Brunswick, birded in temperatures ranging from 0° to 20° and in crested snow ranging from six to eight inches—two hundred forty-two miles by car and more than forty-one miles on foot. A snowmobile was used for two hours to maneuver twelve obviously rugged miles. The group totaled out at thirty-four species and over twenty-five hundred individuals; but alas, they missed a Snowy Owl on count day!

There are (each year I suppose) a few one-man Christmas Bird Counts. In 1979, I understand, there were ten. It has recently been suggested we eliminate counts not attended by at least eight participants (or some "reasonable" number) on the grounds the territory is not being properly/adequately covered. Having done considerable birding alone I have great empathy for the loners.

This Christmas season go out and participate in your local CBC. And in the tradition of Frank Chapman and Clara Weedmark, share a part of your Christmas with the birds.

BIRD LOG
NOTE: *The following birds were spotted by Mr. Bernstein on the birding trip(s) described in this chapter. They are in the order they were sighted.*

OLIVE VIEW MEDICAL CENTER, SYLMAR,
  CALIFORNIA:
Fox Sparrow, *Passerella iliaca*

ANTELOPE VALLEY, AROUND
LANCASTER, CALIFORNIA:
Northern Harrier (Marsh Hawk),
  Circus cyaneus
House Wren, *Troglodytes aedon*
Water Pipit, *Anthus spinoletta*
European Starling, *Sturnus vulgaris*
California Quail, *Callipepla
  californica*
Merlin, *Falco columbarius*
Sharp-shinned Hawk, *Accipiter
  striatus*
Lark Sparrow, *Chondestes grammacus*
Greater Roadrunner, *Geococcyx
  californianus*
Vesper Sparrow, *Pooecetes
  grammineus*
Yellow-rumped Warbler, (Myrtle race),
  Dendroica coronata
Yellow-rumped Warbler (Audubon's
  race), *Dendroica coronata*
Dark-eyed Junco, *Junco hyemalis
  oreganus*
Black Phoebe, *Sayornis nigricans*

Say's Phoebe, *Sayornis saya*
Lincoln's Sparrow, *Melospiza
  lincolnii*
Horned Lark, *Eremophila alpestris*
Ferruginous Hawk, *Buteo regalis*
Golden Eagle, *Aquila chrysaetos*
Sprague's Pipit, *Anthus spragueii*
Sage Thrasher, *Oreoscoptes montanus*
Pine Siskin, *Carduelis pinus*
Prairie Falcon, *Falco mexicanus*
Brewer's Blackbird, *Euphagus
  cyanocephalus*
Brown-headed Cowbird, *Molothrus
  ater*
Long-billed Curlew, *Numenius
  americanus*
Red-breasted Sapsucker, *Sphyrapicus
  ruber*
Red-shouldered Hawk, *Buteo lineatus*
Pectoral Sandpiper, *Calidris
  melanotos*

13.
Identifying Immatures.

FOR MOST BIRDWATCHERS the only birds worth bothering to identify—worth looking at, really—are the adults, preferably in bright spring (alternate) plumage. Anything younger is an identification problem. And who needs more problems?

Pictured in the field guides are the mating plumages of each species, male and female if there is a difference, and usually the male in winter (basic) plumage if that difference is significant. Pictorially, visually, subadult birds of many species have in the field guides been given short shrift—here a glimpse of the head only, there ignored altogether. Still, how much should we expect of a field guide? To provide a likeness of first-year birds, male and female, would lengthen the book to a size unusable in the field. Immature birds have been almost totally ignored more by birdwatchers than by field guide authors. They are one step below fall females. That's the truth of it. So why bother to learn the immies, anyway?

If there is an average of four young birds for each pair of adults flying south after nesting, then you are actually seeing more than twice as many immatures as adult birds in fall migration (realistically, probably four times as many). Which, indeed, makes it a matter of some importance. An immature bird is just as countable as a full adult. By not recognizing it you could be cheating yourself out of some of the harder-to-find species on your life list, year list, or state list. And although for a life bird I have always tried to insist on a mature specimen in its "most beautiful" plumage—the exceptions being, of course, vagrants from other continents, birds of only minor plumage differences, or immatures where mating-plumaged birds are not normally seen in my own particular geographic sphere of birding—this is my own personal idiosyncracy.

More important—and what really bothers me—is a growing awareness that not familiarizing ourselves with the plumages of birds that are less than adult may very well be prejudicing some of the statistical bird count programs.

*

It is five o'clock in the morning when I meet Shum Suffel and Hal Baxter near a freeway offramp for a ride down to San Diego's Point Loma, a rather famous bird trap, on the trail of one of the most wanted birds in North America, the Connecticut Warbler. Word has it there was one immature present the week previous (both Hal and Shum had gone down for that one), but that one had no tail, and consequently I did not bother to "chase" it. Now, however, there are supposedly two birds of that species present, the most recently arrived with a tail!

It is October 14, 1980, and we are on the scene by 7:45 A.M. We are scouting the Naval Cemetery when I spot a warbler in a low tree beside the administration building and whisper hoarsely. "Warbler at two o'clock in the laurel tree!"

The only other time I had met up with a Connecticut Warbler prior to this was May 4, 1979, in the Fort Jefferson courtyard on the Dry Tortugas. That was a male with a full white eye ring showing through a solid gray face and breast covering. So this bird on Point Loma, California, really surprises me. Although I know one should expect only an immature on the West Coast at this time of year, I do not have the picture of a juvenile in mind. I am looking forward to seeing—tell the truth and shame the devil!—a fat olive-green-backed, yellow-bellied bird with dark gray breast and hood and full white eye ring.

What I see is this chunky bird that exposes its front as it feeds, probably on aphids, from leaves on the twig to which it clings. It has a whitish throat, the mere suggestion of a buff-gray breast, and pale yellow on the belly and undertail coverts. Ah, there's the key. This species has exceptionally long undertail coverts. As its head bends toward me I view a pale gray-brown cap and face and a thin white eye ring. The back appears buffy tinged with green. The bird flies up, turns and disappears over the hill. We never find it again.

It was a calm little warbler that made not a sound and appeared very unhurried in its feeding, and disappeared. Hal says several times that he saw clearly the edge of the apron between breast and abdomen. No one mentions the length of the undertail coverts—a critical mark here—because probably none of us looked for it. Somewhat disappointed in this impostor, I say very little. Actually what I have seen doesn't really sink in until I write out my notes on the bird and back home find the artist's portrayal of an immature Connecticut Warbler in W. Earl Godfrey's *Birds of Canada* and do a comparison. Only then am I certain this is what we had seen as our first bird of the day! Oh, yes, it was and is. And indeed there are many more like that particular bird seen in fall than there are the adults, the male's hood then being brown and the female being overall more brownish than the male.

Two huge spotlights, one on either side of the cemetery administration building, are left on each night and a good part of the day. This attracts hoards of flying insects to the nearby green viburnum and juniper shrubs. And this explains why this warbler—plus other eastern immies gone astray, their mental compass one hundred eighty degrees awry—stay on here (and in some cases return year after year) instead of flying on to eventual death when they "run out of gas" over the Pacific Ocean.

Just across the way in the very old Montezuma cypresses, together with one Hermit and fifteen Townsend's Warblers (western birds), we discover a Tennessee Warbler. As expected, it is also an immy, with greenish cap and back (the adult male has a gray cap, but the back of both sexes at all ages in all seasons is green) and a yellow-green breast.

Very generally, broadly, and briefly, the plumage sequence of the passerines (song birds) goes this-a-way:

Adults go through a postnuptial (after-nesting) molt when all feathers, both contour and flight feathers, are replaced, leaving them in winter (basic) dress. In some species this is when the males look very much like the drab females. This "complete" molt may be lengthy, usually commencing even as the young are fledged from the nest and occasionally continuing to the time of arrival on southern wintering grounds. The following spring, prior to commencement of mating, most undergo a "partial" molt when they replace some or all of their head and body feathers. In many species the color changes are quite drastic (i.e., the Scarlet Tanager). In others the same-color feather is molted so the only difference is the fact the bird looks fresher with unworn plumage.

The male Indigo Bunting emerges from a month-long late summer molt looking very, very buffy-brown. The exciting blue dress it wears when it returns in the spring is not exclusively the result of feathers being replaced during the spring prenuptial molt but is also due to the wearing away over the long winter of the buffy-brown feather tips, revealing the exquisite blue feathering just below the surface. The wearing away of feather tips plays a significant role in color change in many species. And as with some of the other passerines, the immature male will not wear fully adult plumage in its first nesting season. The full-blown indigo plumage will not be seen until the following spring.

The male House Sparrow wears away the gray feather tips of its winter plumage to reveal the back bib and crown characteristic of that species. (If you've wondered why the House Sparrow is so common and so ubiquitous, it may help to know that J.K. Terres says the females are ready to lay eggs at eight weeks of age!) And the winter male Snow Bunting looks quite brown only because his white feathering is brown-tipped. By late spring, these feather ends worn away, our strikingly black and white Snow Bunting appears again in the more familiar costume.

Meanwhile, back at the ranch nest. The newborn bird goes from natal down to nestling plumage, and at about the time it leaves the nest it undergoes, as its parents achieve their postnuptial molt, its "hatch-year" or juvenile plumage, which in some cases is actually winter plumage for the species; but there is wide variation. Among some sparrows, for example, "junior" in just a few months looks very similar to the parents.

Broadly speaking, shorebirds arrive on their northern mating territories in full nuptial regalia and change into winter plumage as they arrive or after they arrive on their wintering grounds. Thus, the shorebirds in neat clean plumage seen in North America in autumn are all juveniles. Their parents, which precede their young in migrating, are the birds with the worn ragged feathers—they may have already started molting. A particular exception is the Dunlin, which waits for the other shorebirds to leave the far north breeding grounds before it also departs. But because it is such a late migrant it molts in new feathering before migrating south.

Among long-billed waders such as Black-necked Stilt and Avocet the length of the bill is helpful in distinguishing between the young and the adult of the species, inasmuch as the bill grows to its optimum as the bird matures. Thus, if you spot an Avocet with a dainty, upturned short bill—one that looks shorter than the others around it—you may know you are looking at a young bird.

The observant among you are already familiar with the markings to be looked for in picking out the "youngsters," or birds of the year, among the passerines. The spotting on the breast of the robin juvy is easily recognized and learned. This does not mean that spotting on any bird makes it a young bird. Not by any means. Starlings, remember, are highly speckled in their winter plumage. One very striking example, though, of a young bird that is freckled with white spots over the head and down the front of its body—quite bizarre when viewed side by side with its parent—is the Townsend's Solitaire. Only its silhouette even suggests a solitaire!

To pick out the immatures, look for—very broadly, now—a plumage the reverse of that of the adult. That is, if the adult has a streaked breast, often the juvy will present a clear breast, and vice versa. Look for mottling and/or brown streaking, especially on the breast, and look for much brown feathering, especially in gulls. For a few weeks the Killdeer junior has only one band rather than the adult's two across the white breast. The largest birds—eagle, albatross, condor—require several years of slow changing before they come into adult plumage, which is ordinarily the signal that they are ready for mating. It is at least five years, and possibly up to ten, before the Bald Eagle comes into its white head and tail, and approximately five years also before the Golden Eagle loses the white in its tail and wings and darkens into full adulthood. It takes a five-year span for the condor to finally show the white triangles along the leading edges of the wings, indicating its mating-readiness, and this, of course, further complicates the heroic attempts to maintain the tiny population still extant. But don't bother looking for immature Horned Larks after late summer/early fall, for they reach adulthood, according to J. Van Tyne and A. Berger, after post-juvenile molt at about three months of age!

Our gulls range from two to four years in reaching full adult plumage: the larger the gull, the greater the number of years required. The key in gulls as indicators of age, or specifically, lack of age, is brown feathering. This is true as well of many hawks.

The hatch-year Wood Stork, unlike its parents, has a conspicuous yellow bill, and to make it even easier to distinguish between them, the adults present gray bald heads. The adult Great Blue Heron has an all-black crown while the young one has a white streak over the top of its head.

The Summer Tanager I saw along the Southern California coast January 28, 1982 was one of the wierdest looking birds I had ever spotted. It was mottled with dull red on the head and back, with green on the wings and tail, and blotchy yellowish underparts. It was, of course, an immature, either male or red-phased female. It looked as if it had the chicken pox and yellow jaundice. But my concern was unnecessary; I'm sure it was wearing its "normal" and most beautiful dress by spring.

On this same day at Harbor Lake in Long Beach, California, Jon Dunn and I found the reported immature Mourning Warbler. The discoverer of this bird, Mitch Heindel, says he thought for a week or so that he was looking at a female Common Yellowthroat! In truth, it could more easily have been identified as an immature MacGillivray's Warbler. A most difficult identification problem would be between young Mourning and MacGillivray's Warblers. This particular bird was the worst kind of skulker, but early morning it would show itself. Its head, back, and tail were olive-green. It had just the shadow of a gray hood and breast band over yellow underparts from the chin down to and including its long undertail coverts. A Mourning Warbler with a yellow throat! The bill was slightly decurved and heavier than that of a Common Yellowthroat. Its glossy black eye was surrounded with what seemed to me a thin, pale gray, broken eye ring. From time to time it would give its single call. *Chwit!*

The Eastern Phoebe in fresh fall plumage is not white but yellow down the front, as are the young, and this gets dingy and wears off as the year moves on. The all-black hatch-year Heermann's Gull will in three years, in breeding plumage, end up with an immaculate white head and a red bill. The Red-eyed Vireo has brown eyes in its first year. The Common Grackle juvenile is gray with sooty-brown eyes which will not turn to yellow until the fall. The greenish first year male Scarlet Tanager that leaves in the fall will next spring return as a scarlet beauty! And, by first spring, the brown-headed young will turn into a real Red-headed Woodpecker, its appearance fitting its name.

The study of immature birds is fascinating and can be very useful. It makes birdwatching more interesting, and will certainly add the weight of knowledgeable birding to the statistical counts. And, as I trust anyone will plainly see, it does tend to prove there just may be something redeeming about the younger generation after all!

BIRD LOG

NOTE: *The following birds were spotted by Mr. Bernstein on the birding trip(s) described in this chapter. They are in the order they were sighted.*

POINT LOMA, CALIFORNIA:
Connecticut Warbler, *Oporornis agilis*
Hermit Warbler, *Dendroica occidentalis*
Townsend's Warbler, *Dendroica townsendi*
Tennessee Warbler, *Vermivora peregrina*

HARBOR LAKE, LONG BEACH, CALIFORNIA:
Mourning Warbler, *Oporornis philadelphia*

14.
California, Here I Come.

EACH YEAR we spend some of the spring and all of summer among the ruggedly beautiful "hills 'n' hollers" of West Virginia, and though the birding is exciting and, of course, completely different, I confess that all the while I am enjoying the lush green forests and the eastern avifauna I am haunted with a yearning for the salt-sprayed birds of Malibu. That name is, for me, not a residential hideaway for Hollywood stars, but a showplace for birds—some star-quality birds.

October 16, 1982, just three days after arriving back in southern California, I am at Malibu Lagoon. At 6:30 the sun comes up in the eastern sky looking like a forest fire, all red and orange and gold. Driving here through Malibu Canyon was saddening. Fire had just a few days ago swept through the hills, leaving only charred stumps, gray ash, and the acrid smell of smoke in the air. Although horrified, from personal experience over many years, I know this happens on an almost regular basis and that both the hills and the wildlife are only temporarily set back, and will survive.

On the asphalt parking lot I find Brewer's Blackbirds, a western species which is moving east rapidly, and greet them like long-lost friends. It has been five months! Hal Ferris, my birding buddy, is not here yet, so I bird around while waiting. Crows overhead. What is in the creek? Coots. I am even glad to see western mud hens. Along the near edge of the creek are two wary Black-bellied Plovers. They take a few steps, stop stock-still, cautiously look about, pick at some bits of food in the sand, take a few steps, stop again, and so on. They are like windup toys.

Flying in formation is a flock of Western Sandpipers, and with them a single Least Sandpiper, brown-bibbed and so much smaller. They drop as one on a sand bar and commence feeding. *Kill-deee! Kill-deee!* comes from across the stream. Four of the "prisoner-striped" birds are fussing about near the rocky edge. Ah, a Semi-palmated Plover with the single band across the breast. It reminds me of the Mongolian Plover which was found just north of here a few weeks back and which I missed while still in the east. Poor Chuck, never there when the good birds are there! Two more Semipalms are pottering along the sandy bank; and fishing up the creek, silent and motionless, so very patient, his long spear at the ready, a Great Blue Heron.

Across from me now in the low brush are two Black-crowned Night-Herons, showing the white fronts of fully matured birds, their red eyes making it appear they've been up all night, and they no doubt have, but not playing gin rummy. They stand hunched over as if in a stupor. Overhead a second-year Ring-billed Gull looks down on me, followed by a brown California first-year Gull.

Close to the viaduct under which the tidal water flows and over which passes traffic along Pacific Coast Highway, there is a gull with a thin greenish bill, a Mew Gull! Oh it is so very nice to be back home! I breathe in deep gulps of the clean salt air.

From the castor bean and mule fat plants near the viaduct I hear the *Kwep!* call of the Song Sparrow, and then the querulous, ascending violin-string calls of both American and Lesser Goldfinches. They fly out of the brush and upstream, the American showing the white rump and undertail coverts that sets him apart from the Lesser. Except for the lower belly on an occasional female, the Lesser Goldfinches are yellow-rumped and yellow-bellied. In winter plumage, the American's very wide wingbars are distinctive, on the male the upper bar is yellow. A drab female Anna's Humming-bird hovers over the red-flowering bottlebrush. It is 7:00. Where is Hal? Southern California traffic, no doubt! The sun is well up and very bright. A Western Meadowlark skims like Batman with spread cape into the weedy patch at the edge of the channel, then pops up and turns to show me its jet-black "V" on the brilliant yellow breast.

I get my scope from the car and set it up. Far upstream there are Mallard Ducks. A gray bird—a Willet—teeters along on dark green legs. As if from a diving board, a Black Phoebe flies from a point of rock at stream-side into acrobatic flycatching, finally returning to its exact take-off spot on the point of rock, its white belly glinting in the sun. A Spotted Sandpiper in winter plumage dips and teeters and wriggles, then flies off crazily, as if trying to go in two directions at once. A female Belted Kingfisher noisily clatters downstream, showing her rufous bellyband. A pair of Blue-gray Gnatcatchers, the stuntmen of the bird world, dive headlong into a bush nearby, full steam ahead!

At 7:15 Hal Ferris appears, and the heavy flow of traffic along Pacific Coast Highway is sufficient explanation for his tardiness. We walk under the viaduct toward the ocean and the lagoon. The tide has started out, but it is still too high, and the hoped-for display of a vast array of gulls on the sandbars is left for later.

What has happened to the Savannah Sparrow field?!

Men and equipment are at work. They have torn out all vegetation and leveled the wild area, creating a wildlife sanctuary where birders may watch shorebirds from raised short wooden bridges across several narrow fingerlike tidal inlets.

It will probably take several years before the raw and naked look is covered by plantings that look as if they belong. Still, the long battle waged by so many, including the Los Angeles Audubon Society, to "Save Malibu Lagoon" has, it would appear, finally been won. It was a six-year war. The conservationists found themselves stymied by—of all things—the local Little League, which used part of the area for baseball diamonds. Over the years lawsuits cannonaded back and forth. The Little Leaguers, with professional political help, were marched in uniform through the courtroom and before the television cameras at the office of the governor in Sacramento to assert their claim. Often there was not, as the saying goes, a dry eye in the house.

But all the tears dried when, just a few months ago, the State Parks Department purchased land and relocated the youthful baseball players. And although every bit of the dust has still not settled, the plans for restoration of the marsh at Malibu Lagoon are underway—a heartening success for those who must continue to speak out for the birds, inasmuch as the birds cannot speak out for themselves and have no standing in a court of law.

In the lagoon, there are Pied-billed and Eared Grebes—gray-throated—and some very dark Heermann's Gulls with black-tipped red bills, some even darker with flesh-colored black-tipped bills indicating hatch-year birds. Many of the gulls here are post-breeding wanderers up from Mexico.

"Elegant Tern!" I yell, and we eagerly watch, among the many black-billed, black-eyelined Forster's Terns, the single bird with a long yellow bill flashing in the sunlight. Lucky to find this tern. The Elegants having been here since midsummer, will, in the main, have flown south by Thanksgiving, and all will be gone by December.

Now we turn to look west at the ocean—"my" ocean. The tide is almost imperceptibly ebbing. Sunlight shows green through the waves that start as whispers at the surf line and grow in size and speed and volume until, frothy whitecaps falling over their faces, in an explosive roar they smash themselves on the beach and are sucked back to the sea making gentle gurgling sounds. And between the rhythmic rising and falling of each wave, pale gray Sanderlings dance and feed. Nimble as wraiths they scramble down on the very edge of the waterline to pick-pick-pick in the wet sand, then turn and, the following wave licking at their heels, scramble back up the beach. The Sanderlings now in winter plumage are even paler than the pale buff Snowy Plovers, tiniest of the shorebirds, that skitter about as if on ball bearings over equally pale buff sand, so that one must look twice to see them at all!

At one end of the beach washed over time and again by the waves, I stare at the black rocks. Was that a rock that moved?! There, again it moves! It is a Black Turnstone, and closer observation reveals several are feeding here, again in natural camouflage!

We focus the scope on the edge of the lagoon to the south. More Black Turnstones, oh, and Ruddy Turnstones, those with bright orange legs. A Willet and a Black-bellied Plover walk together and stop together. Far offshore we spy five Brandt's Cormorants, heavy-necked and short-tailed, flying south. On the anchored raft in the sea among many Brown Pelicans, the large crook-necked Double-crested, and a single thin-billed, thin-necked Pelagic Cormorant! Those are the three cormorants we expect here.

Western Grebes, white-throated, bob majestically on the water near the base of the Malibu Pier. "Marbled Godwits!" Two drop in just beyond the sand dune at the south end of the lagoon. Two Common Ravens, wedge-tailed, fly over making raucous noises, and then from overhead the high-pitched calls of Water Pipits. *Pipit! Pipit!*

We walk south to the rear of what is an elegant residence acquired by Los Angeles County and rented in recent years by nearby Pepperdine University for use of its president, but soon to become a public park. There is a Say's Phoebe, persimmon-bellied, on the back fence, then Orange-crowned Warblers, one after another—we count fourteen! Some are bright yellow all down the front (the race *lutescens* that breeds in British Columbia and its islands) and many very grayish (the "eastern" race *celata* that breeds almost all across Canada) both of which move down the West Coast in fall, the immatures even grayer than their parents.

The Starlings, in spotted winter dress, are striking. Many of the Yellow-rumped (Audubon's) Warblers, although they have lost the yellow spots on flanks, nape and throat, still show the yellow rumps. In the colorful courtyard, heavily planted, we find a pair of Bewick's Wrens, and though I look for it, I see no trace of white along the edges of the tail because the outer tail feathers are folded in.

There are White-crowned Sparrows and a Lincoln's, gray-faced, just below a Song Sparrow, so we may compare how much heavier the breast-streaking is on the latter. And though the central breast spot cannot be ignored, inasmuch as all three *Melospiza* sparrows—Song, Lincoln's, and immature Swamp—may show the spot, depending on the arrangement of their feathering, and all three pump their rounded tails in flight, more than these two characters should be looked for to identify them. Drat! Then how can one tell what's what? The Lincoln's is grayer, and the Swamp is darker and redder than the Song. The heaviness of the breast streaking, the color behind the facial pattern, the caps, and the songs and calls are all ways of distinguishing them in the field.

Monarch butterflies are abundant and fill some of the trees. A male Wilson's Warbler has almost completely covered his black cap with yellow pollen. A Willow Flycatcher, small, very white underneath, showing two narrow white wing bars and a thin white eye ring, poses momentarily on a twig, then disappears behind the leaves of the tree. This one is moving south, but he is a late migrant. We watch, amazed, a mockingbird call *Chicago! Chicago!* in imitation of the California Quail. I can scarcely believe my eyes. Here on the coast I've heard them imitating many calls, but never quail before. I wonder if the Mockingbird comes from the foothills back of us—of course, the fire displaced this bird!

Here is a Chipping Sparrow with its red cap, showing its black transocular stripe under the white superciliary. Some Chippies winter along the coast. A Brown Towhee walks along the top of the stucco wall, and a Scrub Jay swoops in to show its brown saddle before diving into the high shrubbery filled with the twinkling of busy Bushtits. I am back in California!

Leaving Malibu Lagoon we do the small ponds on the Pepperdine campus, where we add a Wilson's Phalarope—the only phalarope with no wingbar—five Pectoral Sandpipers, a Greater Yellowlegs, a pair of Snowy Egrets, a Cattle Egret, two Common Snipe, a Common Loon, a House Wren, a flock of Horned Larks, a Red-shouldered Hawk, and Savannah Sparrows showing the fine streaking over the cap and the yellowish face.

North up the coast we bird Bonsall Road, where we find a distinctive male Townsend's Warbler—black marks against bright yellow—Rufous-sided Towhees, and both Nuttall's and Acorn Woodpeckers, the latter sounding off like a man sawing wood. Across the way at the south end of Zuma Beach we explore the seven-foot high fennel forest to get out the Lesser Goldfinches and Ruby-crowned Kinglets with their odd-shaped eye ring. A pair of Marsh Wrens reacts excitedly to my Screech Owl call, as well as a Common Yellowthroat, and from the stands of cattails explode families of Red-winged Blackbirds.

Hal turns the scope over to me saying, "Hey, there's a loon out there just opposite the black dog!" I find that kind of direction to a bird hilarious. Far across the beach I spy a black dog galloping full-out down the shore. "Opposite the black dog, indeed!" However, I do find a Common Loon out there, I tell him, "just under the four

Elegant Terns." Elegants are everywhere. From the hillside across the way comes the popcorn-machine laughter of a Wrentit.

A bit farther north we are birding Leo Carillo Beach. It is 1:30 P.M. and the ocean with bright sun on it is blue but covered with silver spangles. Here are more Willets, Sanderlings, Western Gulls—and a movie company! We have blundered onto the filming of the very last episode of the TV series "M.A.S.H." This segment, we learn, will be shown in February of 1983. This is a beach scene with Jamie Farr, the little guy who occasionally dresses up in female clothing, doing a barbecue on the beach. Hordes of people brought out here on location to help with the filming are milling about, and with binoculars and scope, unkempt in old birding clothes, we blend in perfectly. They probably think we're checking background and camera angles!

It must be in the nineties now—in mid-October! Where else but in southern California would birdwatchers come across something like this? I love it!

BIRD LOG

NOTE: *The following birds were spotted by Mr. Bernstein on the birding trip(s) described in this chapter. They are in the order they were sighted.*

MALIBU LAGOON, CALIFORNIA:

Brewer's Blackbird, *Euphagus cyanocephalus*
American Crow, *Corvus brachyrhynchos*
American Coot, *Fulica americana*
Black-bellied Plover, *Pluvialis squatarola*
Western Sandpiper, *Calidris mauri*
Least Sandpiper, *Calidris minutilla*
Semipalmated Plover, *Charadrius semipalmatus*
Black-crowned Night-Heron *Nycticorax nycticorax*
Ring-billed Gull, *Larus delawarensis*
California Gull, *Larus californicus*
Mew Gull, *Larus canus*
Song Sparrow, *Melospiza melodia*
American Goldfinch, *carduelis tristis*
Lesser Goldfinch, *Carduelis psaltria*
Anna's Hummingbird, *Calypte anna*
Western Meadowlark, *Sturnella neglecta*
Willet, *Anas platyrhynchos*
Mallard, *catoptrophorus semipalmatus*
Black Phoebe, *Sayornis nigricans*
Spotted Sandpiper, *Actitis maculara*
Belted Kingfisher, *Ceryle alcyon*
Blue-gray Gnatcatcher, *Polioptila caerulea*
Pied-billed Grebe, *Podilymbus podiceps*
Eared Grebe, *Podiceps nigricollis*
Heermann's Gull, *Larus heermanni*
Elegant Tern, *Stema elegans*
Forster's Tern, *Sterna forsteri*
Sanderling, *Calidris alba*

Snowy Plover, *Charadrius alexandrinus*
Black Turnstone, *Arenaria melanocephala*
Ruddy Turnstone, *Arenaria interpres*
Brandt's Cormorant, *Phalacrocorax penicillatus*
Double-crested Cormorant, *Pelecanus occidentalis*
Pelagic Cormorant, *Phalacrocorax pelagicus*
Brown Pelican, *Phalacrocorax auritus*
Western Grebe, *Aechmophorus occidentalis*
Marbled Godwit, *Limosa fedoa*
Common Raven, *Corvus corax*
Water Pipit, *Anthus spinoletta*
Say's Phoebe, *Sayornis saya*
Orange-crowned Warbler, *Vermivora celata*
European Starling, *Sturnus vulgaris*
Yellow-rumped Warbler, *Dendroica coronata*
Bewick's Wren, *Thryomanes bewickii*
White-crowned Sparrow, *Zonotrichia leucophrys*
Lincoln's Sparrow, *Melospiza lincolnii*
Song Sparrow, *Melospiza melodia*
Wilson's Warbler, *Wilsonia pusilla*
Willow Flycatcher, *Empidonax traillii*
Northern Mockingbird, *Mimus polyglottos*
Chipping Sparrow, *Spizella passerina*
Brown Towhee, *Pipilo fuscus*
Scrub Jay, *Aphelocoma coerulescens*
Bushtit, *Psaltriparus minimus*

PEPPERDINE CAMPUS, MALIBU,
CALIFORNIA:
Wilson's Phalarope, *Phalaropus tricolor*
Pectoral Sandpiper, *Calidris melanotos*
Greater Yellowlegs, *Tringa melanoleuca*
Snowy Egret, *Egretta thula*
Cattle Egret, *Bubulcus ibis*
Common Snipe, *Gallinago gallinago*
Common Loon, *Gavia immer*
House Wren, *Troglodytes aedon*
Horned Lark, *Eremophila alpestris*
Red-shouldered Hawk, *Buteo lineatus*
Savannah Sparrow, *Passerculus sandwichensis*

ZUMA BEACH, CALIFORNIA:
Lesser Goldfinch, *Carduelis psaltria*
Ruby-crowned Kinglet, *Regulus calendula*
Marsh Wren, *Cistothorus palustris*
Common Yellowthroat, *Geothlypis trichas*
Red-winged Blackbird, *Agelaius phoeniceus*
Common Loon, *Gavia immer*
Elegant Tern, *Sterna elegans*
Wrentit, *Chamaea fasciata*

BONSALL ROAD, MALIBU, CALIFORNIA;
Rufous-sided Towhee, *Pipilo erythrophthalmus*
Townsend's Warbler, *Dendroica townsendi*
Nuttall's Woodpecker, *Picoides nuttallii*
Acorn Woodpecker, *Melanerpes formicivorus*

LEO CARRILLO BEACH, CALIFORNIA:
Willet, *Catroptrophorus semipalmatus*
Sanderling, *Calidris alba*
Western Gull, *Larus occidentalis*

15.
Subspecies: Almost the Same But Not Quite.

THE SUBJECT is Song Sparrow. A Song Sparrow is a Song Sparrow is a Song Sparrow. True? Far from true. No more true scientifically than Gertrude Stein's "A rose is a rose is a rose." A casual leafing through your spring garden catalogue will turn up many varieties of the tea rose. And, as with roses, there are dramatic variations in size and coloration and even markings on separate races or subspecies of birds. Subspecies designation recognizes a group within a species which has distinguishable differences as the result of geographical/ecological isolation: these subspecies members can potentially interbreed with other subspecies of their same species.

Take the very common, the ubiquitous, Song Sparrow, *Melospiza melodia*. There are thirty-one subspecies listed in the 1957 checklist of the American Ornithologists Union (AOU). Thanks to Eugene Cardiff of the San Bernardino County Museums, Jon Dunn and I have set out before us a drawerful of bird skins tagged *Melospiza melodia something."* Studying and comparing them is almost as exciting as being out in the field turning up different species of birds. This is indeed a field trip in a desk drawer!

Among the populations from the interior of California there is the subspecies *saltonis*, which is very pale and has very little streaking on

135

the breast. This race is found along the Colorado River and the Salton Sea. Then there is *cooperi*, which nests north of the Los Angeles Basin, much darker on the back, with heavier darker streaking down the front. Dramatic differences. *Saltonis* seems to be disappearing. The theory is that it is being replaced by *cooperi* which, by moving down the Whitewater River into the sea, is rapidly taking over *saltonis* habitat.

To the north, in the Owens Valley, just east of and in the shadow of Mt. Whitney, the highest peak in our Sierra Nevadas, the Song Sparrow is of the *fisherella* subspecies, its back darker than *saltonis* on the breast. From nesting grounds in the extreme northwest corner of the United States there is the race *montana*, which winters from Death Valley to Mexico and is probably the dominant Song Sparrow in winter in the eastern part of southern California away from *cooperi*. The race *merrilli* that breeds as far south as extreme northeast California is somewhat darker and redder on the back and in its breast-streaking than the *montana*.

Of the coastal subspecies there is *heermanni* which breeds in the Sacramento Valley, also north of the L.A. Basin, as does *cooperi*, but is slightly darker even than *cooperi*. In truth, as we go north along the coast the races get both larger and darker, and they tend to be more and more migratory, with the exception of the Aleutian types. Resident in northwest California one finds *cleonensis*, and farther north the race *morphna*, which is very dark and rufescent and has much gray on the underparts.

From outside of California, almost as pale as *saltonis* is the subspecies *fallax* from southern Arizona; and from the opposite coast, one of the eastern subspecies is the nominate race *melodia*, which breeds from southeastern Canada to Virginia and winters as far south as the tip of Florida. This race is not too different from the dark-backed *cooperi* dorsally but is a bit buffer on the breast and has finer and paler streaking.

The topper, found on the outer Aleutian Islands, is *maxima*, largest of all the Song Sparrows—as large as a Wood Thrush, actually—easily one-third larger than the tiny *saltonis* we started this "trip" with, and much much darker by far.

Learning the subspecies can be fun. Merely making a stab at it will make birding less of a mystery. Being aware of the full range of geographical variation enables a birdwatcher to understand members of a species better and more easily identify them.

Every day you witness these shades of variation both seasonally and geographically, and the more precise your observations—even when possible, as to subspecies—the greater value they have. Knowledge of such variation, of course, leads to a clearer picture of migration patterns and bird distribution and to a better comprehension of how and why subspecies evolve. Indeed, it certainly makes for an increased appreciation of birds.

Recent changes by both the AOU and ABA have resulted in leaving only the Wood Thrush in the genus *Hylocichla*; all other North American thrushes are now in *Catharus*.

Flank color is critical in identifying *Catharus* thrushes. All western races of the Hermit thrush have gray or grayish-brown flanks as contrasted to the eastern subspecies, such as *faxoni*, which have lighter and buffier rather than grayish flank coloring. Aside from the Rocky Mountain race, which is larger, western Hermits are on the average smaller in size than their eastern cousins.

Of the Hermit Thrushes that breed in California, the subspecies *slevini* is the palest both dorsally and ventrally of all races of that species. They winter primarily in Mexico. The Hermit Thrushes we see in California in winter are mainly out of Alaska; are all of the nominate *guttata* group; are, of course, gray; have dark dorsal coloration and fairly dark spotting on the breast (the buff on the breast being pale) by comparison to eastern subspecies, and are darker than *slevini*. By mid-April, certainly by May 1, most *guttatas* have gone north to Alaska and their breeding grounds and back come *slevini*!

The largest and grayest of all western Hermit Thrushes are the subspecies *sequotensis* and *Auduboni*, which breed in the eastern Sierras, the high mountains of southern California, and all through the Rockies, including southeast Arizona. Compared to *slevini*, the breast spots are larger and darker and the overall color is slightly grayer. These two races winter in central and southern Mexico.

It was long presumed, and still is by many western birdwatchers, that the Hermit Thrush seen both winter and summer was the same one and that this species, in altitudinal migration, went up the mountain to breed in spring and moved back down the mountain in fall. It was only the concentrated study of subspecies that showed clearly that in California and Arizona (and no doubt in many other places) we are seeing different subspecies winter and summer!

There are two subspecies of the Gray-cheeked Thrush and three of the Veery. They all have gray flanks, as do all western races of the Hermit Thrush. Of Swainson's Thrushes, the eastern race *swainsoni* and the *almae* branch of the subspecies from the Rocky Mountains and the Great Basin have brownish-gray flanks and an olive cast to the upper parts. It was *swainsoni* that was previously called the Olive-backed Thrush. The most common Pacific coast Swainson's Thrush, *ustulatus*, is much redder dorsally and has buffy flanks. The other Pacific coast Swainson's Thrush, *oedicus*, is less red dorsally and less buffy on the flanks; which all goes to point up the importance of flank color. When an eastern birder comes to California and sees one of our very bright reddish Swainson's Thrushes, *ustulatus*, he may very well call it a Veery. This mistake is commonplace. Yet a Veery or a Gray-cheeked Thrush in California could only be a vagrant.

The loral spot on the head of a bird is between the eye and the upper mandible. Above that is the anterior supercilium. It is this anterior supercilium as well as the eye ring that is buffy in all Swainson's Thrushes, eastern and western—a buffy line from the buffy eye ring forward to the base of the beak. On Hermit Thrushes the eye ring is whitish. Of course, if the thrush you find has a complete eye ring it has to be either a Swainson's or a Hermit. A Veery or a Gray-cheeked Thrush would show at most only half an eye ring at the back of the eye.

The variations between subspecies are in many cases very obvious even to the naked eye. Two of many examples are the difference between the recently lumped eastern Baltimore and western Bullock's Orioles, now subspecies of Northern Oriole; and the White-winged, Slate-colored, Gray-headed, and Oregon Juncos, now mere races of the Dark-eyed Junco. In other instances the distinctions may be so subtle that they are indistinguishable without having the bird in hand. I cannot stress too strongly the importance of being extremely cautious and critical of identifications of subspecies.

Even as ornithologists learn more about geographical distribution of species and subspecies, boundaries are constantly albeit imperceptibly shifting and changing. Furthermore, some subspecies are as yet poorly defined, for example, the Bald Eagle; to determine whether an individual is the southern version, *Haliaeetus leucocephalus leuco-cephalus*, the "smaller," or *H. l. alascanus*, the "larger" northern Bald Eagle, the bird has to be measured in hand.

Often, in point of fact, a birder must admit to "a probable" identification of a subspecies rather than risk a wrong one. The very meticulous magazine *British Birds*, when reporting on a rare race, says only, "A bird showing the characters of..." Be cautious, but make an attempt certainly, to identify at least as to subspecies group.

One of the advantages of keeping records of subspecies seen in the field, of course, is that one never knows when a subspecies will be split and recognized as a full species of its own. The Yellow-footed Gull, now totally distinct and countable from the Western Gull, is but a recent example. Some birders feel there may be an eventual reversal of the lumped orioles one day; and there is always the possibility that the light and dark races of the Western Grebe will be split, as well as the two subspecies of western Black-tailed Gnatcatchers, *lucida* and *californica*.

To a great extent subspecies evolve through geographical isolation. Because of the diversified topography, there are more isolating barriers in the West than in the East, and, as a result, far more subspecies. Because most field guides are published in the East, western birders feel there is a remarkable prejudice toward, in virtually every species, the depiction of eastern as opposed to western subspecies.

Most of the popular field guides are rife with examples of why western birders are upset. Here are a few: Only the eastern nominate *bellii* race is shown for Bell's Vireo, but in the West one finds the gray *pusilla* and *arizonii* races, quite different from the bright green and yellow eastern subspecies. Only the eastern version of the Solitary Vireo, *solitarius*, showing a blue-gray head and bright yellow flanks, and the gray Rocky Mountain *plumbeus* race are depicted in the field guides. The western subspecies *cassinii* is not shown at all. It is a smaller olive-colored bird lacking the distinct blue on the head as well as the bright yellow on the flanks. In some of the books the adult robin is painted with showy white corners to the tail, obviously

Turdus migratorius migratorius, the eastern race. Though both western subspecies, *propinquus* and *caurinus,* have white tail corners, they are much less marked and much less noticeable.

Surely, eastern birdwatchers have reason to be upset as well. On that coast there are two subspecies of Short-billed Dowitchers. In breeding plumage (when distinctions in plumage are most apparent) the *Limnodromus griseus hendersoni* has a chestnut or chestnut-buff belly and is lightly spotted, if at all, on the breast. The nominate race, *L. g. griseus,* has a white belly and is heavily spotted on its chestnut breast.

Inasmuch as the popular field guides show no distinction between these two races, nor even mention *hendersoni,* but do depict the Long-billed Dowitcher with chestnut breast and belly, unwary birdwatchers who come upon flocks of Shortbills, both subspecies being present (and this is quite common), are led to believe they are looking not at two races of Shortbills but at different species, namely, Short-billed and Long-billed Dowitchers! In the West the single subspecies of Short-billed Dowitcher, *L. g. caurinus,* is, of course, also unmentioned in popular field guides, and though it is somewhere between the two eastern races in spotting and coloring—closer usually to *griseus*— little has been done to dispel the confusion.

Being aware of subspecies, carrying with you the knowledge that you are not seeing merely species but, at different times of the year and in different places, viewing different subspecies is both exciting and challenging. Birders interested in learning subspecies will be disappointed, as I was, to hear that the updated AOU checklist does not list subspecies. Because the AOU is for the first time listing all species, down to and including Middle (Central) America, there will be no room for listing races. In any event, anyone interested should purchase a copy of the 1957 fifth edition of the AOU checklist, which contains all subspecies recognized at the time of publication.

The possibility of seeing different subspecies summer and winter is exciting. Which of those "trash birds" have been deceiving you? Is your "resident" Song Sparrow a migrant being replaced each fall by a subspecies from farther north? You may find out by taking careful note of color, size, and markings of even the most common birds in your summer garden and doing a comparison with your wintering birds.

A visit (by prearrangement) with your notes to a bird skin collection at a natural history museum or at the ornithology department of a university can be very helpful. The science department of your local college should be able to direct you to the nearest bird skin collection.

To the hit 'n' run birdwatcher the members of a species will all look the same. To the careful birder some may perhaps for the first time look almost the same. That is not the same.

(My comments on field guide problems do not apply in whole to the 1983 National Geographic field guide.

I am grateful to Eugene Cardiff, identified above, Alan Wormington, Point Pelee naturalist, and John Dunn for reviewing this chapter and for suggesting invaluable changes in it from the back seat of a bumpy little car en route from a glorious day of birding the Salton Sea.)

16.
The White Wagtail
and the Gray Tailwag.

"AARF! AARF!"

A small gray bird pops up, flies perhaps fifty feet, and drops back down into the sagebrush.

Its head extended, the ears flying pendants, its tail a dirty, tattered flag stretched to the rear, a scruffy gray dog races through the dense, prickly undercover of desert scrub.

Aarf! Aarf! Aarf! The dog is exuberant at re-finding the bird, which again takes flight.

"Oh, shaddup! That's not the bird we're after. You've seen dozens of Black-throated Sparrows before!

The dog scurries wildly back, close enough to brush against the leg of its master, circles away, and, *R-r-raarf!* is off again in another direction.

This is an almost verbatim conversation between Pinto, the dog, and Guy McCaskie, the master. It happened in the Lucerne Valley on May 13, 1978, the day we saw the very rare Cassin's Sparrow in California, which had first been sighted there a day or so before. I was present and witnessed both the conversation and the vagrant sparrow. I am still not sure which impressed me most.

And, typically (I would later learn), it was not until we were all

143

back in the car, Pinto on the rear seat between another birder and me, that this remarkable—and inconsiderate—quadruped, his legs much too short for his body, contorted himself into a pretzel figure and commenced vigorously scratching to rid himself of all the fleas, ticks, spiders, and mites accumulated on his recent desert adventure—by flinging them onto us, or so it appeared to me.

♫

On November 6, 1982 such a long line of birdwatchers has converged on the Los Angeles River near the Willow Avenue bridge in Long Beach that it looks like a run on the bank. From afar the many tripods holding telescopes look like oil drilling rigs, and such a scene can only be a wildcat oil field gone berserk or an ABA (American Birding Association) convention. It is 7:00 A.M., and I know a gusher has not come in yet, for the scopes are unmanned.

I am in time, then, for the scheduled return of Los Angeles County's first wagtail. Alas, the bird being an immature—gray-backed with a black necklace rather than a bib—it cannot be distinguished between the recently split White Wagtail *(Motacilla alba ocularis)*, a breeder in Siberia, St. Lawrence Island, and points on the Alaskan coast adjacent to the Bering Strait, and the newly adopted species of Black-backed Wagtail *(M. lugens)*, a regular visitor from the Kamchatka Peninsula to the outermost Aleutians. Discovered three days ago, the bird was seen briefly just yesterday—but was not seen the day before. One of those!

Here with the other birders is my old friend Pinto, who, having sniffed and carefully marked with upraised leg every projection on and near the bridge, has found his way through the wire-mesh fence to carry out a simply irresistible investigation of the field beyond. And here, too, is our *American Birds* regional editor, Guy McCaskie, permitting his keen eyes to leave the riverbed where the wagtail had previously been found feeding with Water Pipits on the sandbars.

"Pints! C'mon. Pints! Get back here! What are ya doin' out there!? Get back in here and right now!" "Pints" (rhymes with mints) is bellowed with authority and deep affection. Guy turns to me and with fierce pride says, "That dog will always remember the hole he escaped through so he can get back in!"

The small dog, on reaching the other side of the fence, hesitates only a moment, then darts to its left, disappears, and sure enough, just as suddenly reappears on our side of the fence.

"Now you stay here and don't move! Sit! Sit!" At a fast clip the dog slips by us and keeps walking right on up the dike.

𝒥

It gets to be 8:15 A.M. Everybody has said hello to everybody else, and the group is getting restless, wandering back and forth along the dike, still listening and watching, obviously bored with birding a concrete river, waiting for the wagtail to materialize. Yesterday it showed at 9:00 A.M.

This is a shaggy dog story. The difference is this one is mostly true. It is really the saga of an active birdwatcher's dog—"The Perils of Pinto."

Pinto is not a bird dog. He is a birdwatcher. As computed by Guy, with the help of Elizabeth Copper, who just loves the dog, Pinto has more than four hundred species of birds on his California list! "More birds than ninety percent of the birders in the state," according to Liz. "And that," she adds with emphasis, "was as of a couple years ago!" The dog listens and moves in to nuzzle her. She pats him lovingly on the head and says, "He's only short on pelagics!"

Pinto achieved some celebrity on October 19, 1974, when chasing through an alfalfa field in Imperial Beach just south of San Diego he flushed the first California record Sprague's Pipit. Guy's eyes light up when he relates this story, but Jon Dunn in a later interview refines it for me. Jon agrees it was terrific when Pinto flushed the Sprague's the first time, but explains that while everyone was then creeping up on the bird so it could be studied, Pinto broke into a run and flushed it a second time! Whereupon Guy took his celebrity home. The pipit, refound, was ultimately well studied and the record established. Jon says, "no thanks to the dog!"

The mutt has other detractors. Richard Webster calls him simply "Filthy." Not "Simply Filthy," just "Filthy." In describing the gestalt of a bird—or a birdwatcher—Richard never uses two words when one will do.

Those who have spent time with the dog are not evenly divided

among those who praise and those who deprecate him. Kimball
Garrett's tales of Pinto are all negative, as are Jon Dunn's. Still, even
these detractors exchange much-embellished stories about the dog,
always amid gales of laughter, and one senses that beneath the oratory
of presumed loathing they are delighted to have this four-legged
birdwatcher along, if only to be able to tell, the next time they gather,
even more Pinto stories.

The dog admittedly evidences more surface bravado than good
sense. He will challenge any dog that passes, no matter its size or
weight. Once he snarled at a passing German shepherd, which then
simply swept him up into its mouth like a vacuum cleaner. Had the
jaws closed, Pints would have been only a memory. But Pinto gave
his now famous "death rattle," which really means, "Guy, come
quick! Help!" And, fortunately, the master effected another immediate
rescue.

∬

Where the hell is the wagtail? Nine o'clock has come and gone, and it
is now 9:30! Down below on the sandbars I have watched California
and Ring-billed Gulls, a Dunlin, a few Long-billed Dowitchers,
Black-necked Stilts, Avocets, a few Willets, a couple of Black-bellied
Plovers. Water Pipits, four or five at a time, call as they pass overhead
and some drop to the riverbed to walk about, dipping their tails and
picking at food. No wagtail yet!

For a balanced perspective on the dog, don't ask the younger
birders of our area. They'll tell you Pinto will chase any cat until it
turns and faces him, at which time Pints suddenly acts as if the cat is
not there at all! Twice he was fought off by other animals who nipped
his nose: once in the Tijuana River Valley by a mouse, and once in the
water along the dikes of the salt works south of San Diego by a
cornered rabbit!

This dogged little birdwatcher is a cockapoo type, probably mixed
with poodle and dachshund plus other breeds, and, Guy adds, "water
rat or muskrat!" He is a good swimmer, and some say "a yippee little
dog." Elizabeth says, "He's a fine dog, and he leads an exciting life!"

One day at Furnace Creek Ranch in Death Valley Pinto went
charging after a coyote and disappeared in the desert wilds for over an

hour. He came loping back side by side with the coyote. They acted very friendly. And ever since, birders who go to the area have been on the lookout for a Pintote or a Payotee!

His unflagging curiosity and feisty ego have led the dog down some dangerous paths. One time near Oasis at Cottonwood Creek he was lured off by a seemingly friendly dog. Missing for some three hours while the gang was birdwatching, no one suspected he had been lured to an ambush and set upon by a pack of feral dogs. This was Pinto's closest call with death. The "death rattle" led the birders to the nearly dead Pinto in a gully. It was evident from the trail of blood that the dog had dragged himself, his side ripped open, through the entire valley to locate Guy. He was rushed, of course, to the nearest vet, who hemstitched the pieces together. Miraculously, in a couple of weeks, Pinto was as good as new and literally itching to again go birding.

ℐ

By 10:00 A.M. some birders are already leaving. Birding a river is usually exciting. Mucky banks, walls of green leaves, and the flow of water are attractive to most birds. To the birder water movement alone is interesting. One can "listen" to the rhythm of water motion with the eyes. But the Los Angeles River is different. Most of the year it is dry. Around the time of World War II it was made into a flood control channel, because in winter after heavy rains it can become a raging torrent. That is what created the sandbars. Where I now stand, just south of the Long Beach Freeway, the open conduit is perhaps thirty feet in depth, one hundred yards in width, and—solid concrete. Through a depression in the center of the riverbed a thin ribbon of water, perhaps two feet deep now, runs down to the ocean. To be willing to bird a concrete river you would have to be on the trail of a very special bird. A white-water experience this is not.

On the day after Thanksgiving in 1973 at Deep Springs, California, a band of birders was admiring a Northern Goshawk perched on a fence post when Pinto suddenly spied the bird and went dashing wildly toward it. There was an instant hush, and breathing stopped, while such a silent cloud of curses was called down on that dog that it is said there is still blue-colored sand at that spot in the desert wasteland. Unpredictable as ever, Pinto came to a screeching halt smack in front of the accipiter, cocked his leg, and desecrated the bird's perching post!

Elizabeth claims to have a photograph of Pinto looking through a scope at a Baird's Sandpiper one July day at Salton Sea, in his younger days. She says the dog's absolute favorite birding is looking for Sage Grouse in booming season at Lake Crowley, California. In truth, the dog has participated in many Christmas Bird Counts and is very helpful at flushing bitterns, plovers, and other shorebirds. His name, in fact, has been listed as a participant in CBCs in *American Birds* for several years.

Once in Death Valley in the very dead of night, Mike San Miguel's youngster, having a nightmare, started to scream from the front seat of the car. It was unnerving. Pinto, in the back seat with other birders, awoke in alarm, and when the screaming did not abate he lept over the back of the front seat and out the open window into the darkness of the desert. He was not seen until the following morning, when he returned looking refreshed, the only one of the group ready for another hard day of birding!

✑

By 11:15 A.M. Pinto is as bored and disgruntled as the other birdwatchers, for the wagtail has not appeared. Ah, well, just another unfulfilled bird chase.

Most birders returned and ultimately saw the wagtail. I found it, on my third try, December 20, 1982, according to the lunar calendar of my Chinese friends, still well within the Year of the Dog!

BIRD LOG

NOTE: *The following birds were spotted by Mr. Bernstein on the birding trip(s) described in this chapter. They are in the order they were sighted.*

LUCERNE VALLEY, CALIFORNIA:

Black-throated Sparrow, *Amphispiza bilineata*

Cassin's Sparrow, *Aimophila cassinii*

LOS ANGELES RIVER, LONG BEACH, CALIFORNIA:

California Gull, *Larus californicus*

Ring-billed Gull, *Larus delawarensis*

Dunlin, *Erolia alpina*

Long-billed Dowitcher, *Limnodromus scolopaceus*

Black-necked Stilt, *Himantopus mexicanus*

American Avocet, *Recurvirostra americana*

Willet, *Catoptrophorus semipalmatus*

Black-bellied Plover, *Squatarola squatarola*

Water Pipit, *Anthus spinoletta*

White Wagtail, *Motacilla alba ocularis*, OR Black-backed Wagtail, *Motacilla lugens*

17.
Birding Serials:
The Matinee Changes Daily.

WHEN I WAS A KID we looked forward with a hunger to that best of all days, Saturday. At that time of the world it was the custom—indeed, the civil right!—of every kid in the neighborhood to attend the movie matinee and personally experience yet another chapter of a thrill-filled weekly serial.

There was the high adventure of the hunt, frenzied chases against time, suspense, surprise, frustration, love, romance, comedy—all the elements of a satisfying Saturday matinee. I loved it and still do. At some point along the way it came to me that to the birdwatcher the whole world is a theatre, admission is free, and the serial changes every day! Just as the "continued next week" sign flashed on the screen with our hero dangling from a precipitous cliff face or bound hand and foot on a railroad track, now there is the one bird that got away or the one place we should have looked but didn't, or....In birding there is always another chapter of the serial, so next week we will be back.

At 7:00 A.M. of January 8, 1983 I am hurtling towards my birding day southbound on the Santa Ana Freeway. The sky is rosy in the east and south. I feel great and look forward to the day with relish. We are already eight days into the new year and I haven't been birding for three whole days! Starting my new year list will give each bird I spot, no matter how common, added significance. But there are more than common birds waiting.

I feel a bit like a border policeman, for I am on the trail of two rare trespassers from Mexico; first a reported Thick-billed Kingbird on private property in Orange County's Lemon Heights, then a Rufous-backed Robin in the shrubbery at the Newport Ecology Center in Newport Beach. There I hope also to add to my year list the three-time returned Virginia's Warbler, then I'll go north up the coast to the Huntington Beach Pier for a female King Eider, an adventuress from far over the Canadian border. Next I'll turn inland to the Huntington Beach Central Park where I hope to intercept two invaders from the East Coast, a Philadelphia Vireo and a Black-throated Green Warbler.

∬

Three days prior, I had been studying bird skins at the Los Angeles County Museum of Natural History when Kimball Garrett casually mentioned the Rufous-backed Robin. He said if I were interested to call Shum Suffell for directions to it. Was I interested? It would be a life bird for me! My call to Shum sent me scurrying pell-mell down the museum stairs to my car. I searched under the front seat. Damn! My binoculars were at home. And home is in the opposite direction!

I drove hurriedly to North Hollywood to collect my bins, and at the already traffic-filled hour of 2:30 spun around and raced back south. Ridiculous? Not to me. I've missed birds by waiting for a better time. When I hear of a good bird, I go NOW, if at all possible.

At 3:15 I was at the Ecology Center ready to look for the bird, but this was one chase that ended quickly. Don Robertson from northern California was already there and he was already on the robin.

It was hiding on a redwood limb above us, watchful, wary and silent. During our surveillance it flew twice giving a hushed, squeaky call before dropping behind a curtain of shrubbery and trees. It is much like our own robin but appears larger, has rufous on the back and lightly on the wing coverts, and lacks the familiar white eye ring of our robin. Don is exuberant; this is his 499th California state bird!

∬

As I open my car door at the end of Foothill Road in Lemon Heights at 8:10 I hear *Che-beeek!* and at the top of a tall eucalyptus tree on the side of the road I immediately find a striking yellow-fronted black-backed kingbird. Suspicious that I may be looking at a Cassin's, I set up my scope and identify it as the Thick-billed. Rick Clements with another birder has arrived and we take turns looking at it through his powerful Celestron scope until there is no question as to its identity.

The thick, heavy bill, as compared to the shorter and thinner bills of Cassin's or Western Kingbird, is readily apparent. Whereas Western and Tropical Kingbirds are light-headed and light-breasted, and Cassin's is much darker-headed and darker-chested with a contrasting whitish chin, this Thick-billed Kingbird has a very dark, almost black head and back with a light throat. And the breast and belly are much brighter and more yellow than is shown in the common field guides.

Rick and his friend will follow me to the Rufous-backed Robin. We drive west toward the ocean through a blanket of fog that gets thicker as we approach the coast. At the Ecology Center, on the southeast corner of Newport Beach High School, we find ourselves in a gray, murky cloud. It is 8:50. Visibility is not good at twenty feet. We, of course, do not find the robin immediately. Rick and his birding buddy go off to breakfast "while the fog burns off."

Not more than fifteen minutes later a fog pocket lifts and the gathering birders catch a good look as the skulker flushes into an open willow tree from the impenetrable toyon bushes where it has been feeding on the rich, red berries.

Down in the wash in a tangle of foliage behind a chain-link fence I find the feeding Virginia's Warbler. It responds well to spishing and to an owl call. It is a tiny gray bird with a very wide, white eye ring, a mere tinge of yellow on the breast, and a yellow-green splash on the very short undertail coverts and rump. It flies off at the approach of a group of birdwatchers.

Together with Phil Sayre and his friend, both Los Angeles birders, we caravan to the beach in search now of the King Eider. The closer we get to the shore the heavier the fog. We park the cars and walk. Plodding through the sand we literally have to search for the pier! We walk out on the pier with the sea around us, the cold salt spray on my face is bracing but we cannot see the ocean below us, we can barely make out the wooden planking underfoot. We retreat to return again, after breakfast.

At 11:45 visibility is approximately forty feet and we identify the King Eider with a flock of a dozen Surf Scoters, bobbing like corks on the fitful ocean. From time to time they escape the fog and the gaze of prying people on the pier by diving for their food. Its larger size and distinctive head and bill shape, together with the lighter brown color than the female scoters, identify our bird.

So far, great birding. I have two birds from south of our border with Mexico, one from north of our border with Canada, and a Virginia's Warbler, a mountain breeder of the Great Basin ranges. Now for the eastern vagrants!

We travel east to Central Park where we quickly call out the Black-throated Green Warbler from the tall eucalyptus trees at the entrance to a miniature amphitheatre built into the side of a grassy hill. Responding alertly to my owl call, it comes in low and very close to us. It is a first-year bird. It has a bright green back, light yellow on the face, and yellow on the sides of the vent below the belly.

Now for the Philadelphia Vireo! We walk together, we spread out; we look up at, into, over, under, around and in between every branch and twig in that area of the park. We are, of course, looking for a small bird with yellow breast, even a faint wash of yellow, and a prominent white supercilium over a black eyeline. If it is here it would not be easily overlooked. We come up with the bespectacled Solitary Vireo not previously reported here, plus the more expected birds such as American and Lesser Goldfinches, a Song Sparrow at the pond scolding a Common Moorhen (Gallinule), a Belted Kingfisher, a nest-building Anna's Hummingbird (obviously one who either did too well or too poorly with previous clutches) and several sputtering Ruby-crowned Kinglets. But no Philadelphia Vireo.

At 2:30 I am introduced to Tom Payne and Ed Greaves, birders from Sacramento who have just seen the Rufous-backed Robin and now hope to find the Black-throated Green Warbler, a life bird for Tom. They are en route to the airport to return home. Other birders arrive, including four from San Francisco, and well, you know how it is—I volunteer to show them where I had seen the warbler.

To my surprise, we find the amphitheatre packed with well-dressed people, a portable organ playing "Here Comes the Bride" and a minister performing the rites of an outdoor wedding! But the out-of-town birders are all in a hurry; they have to make their planes.

We try to be as quiet and unobtrusive as possible so as not to disturb the ceremony, but to get the bird out I have to do the Screech Owl. Wanting no part in it, Phil Sayre disappears. To further complicate matters, a singer bursts forth with "Oh, Promise Me!" I am prudently embarrassed but adamant. And the scenario goes something like this:

"Oh, promise me that someday you and I"...(I let go softly with a quavering descending owl call)..."Will take our love together".... "Chuck, get the bird out; I gotta go!"...(I emit a more brazen and frightening Screech Owl call)...'"neath some sky"....The organist glances over at us and plays louder....Tom whispers, "I have to go!"....Glares are cast from the flock of well-groomed wedding celebrants at the somewhat grubby group of birdwatchers, heads back and open-mouthed, spread out before them....Again, "Oh, promise me"....

As the organ gets louder I get braver and throwing caution to the winds whistle a loud, spine-tingling Screech Owl call....And as the minister imparts memorable admonitions to the bride and groom, out comes the warbler! I fix my binoculars on the bird to make certain, and then, as the wedding ring is slipped on her finger, I scream in a hoarse stage whisper, "Black-throated Green Warbler at one o'clock, top of the eucalyptus tree!"

The birders come scrambling from every direction, swelling the chorus of "Oohs" and "Aahs." They are getting good looks at the bird.

And where is Tom? Here is his life bird and Tom is gone! Off in the distance, across the park, I catch sight of two figures, Tom and Ed, hurrying away. It must be them. A girl halfway between us hears my call and is racing back. I yell for her to pass on the news and point toward the two disappearing figures. She takes up the call. I see them turn. I wave frantically. They run all the way back. Breathless, Tom gets his life bird.

And now the bride in a yellow gown and the groom wearing a black tux have come out with the minister for picture taking and the guests are hanging back a moment before starting through the reception line. Somewhat contrite, I start towards the minister to make my apologies. But before I can reach him he accepts a pair of binoculars and is himself studying the warbler. And to my delight, as I reach his side, he says over and over again, "Oh, what a bird! Oh, what a bird!"

All the elements of a most satisfying matinee.

BIRD LOG

NOTE: *The following birds were spotted by Mr. Bernstein on the birding trip(s) described in this chapter. They are in the order they were sighted.*

NEWPORT BEACH, CALIFORNIA:
Virginia's Warbler, *Vermivora virginiae*
Rufous-backed Robin, *Turdus rufopalliatus*

HUNTINGTON BEACH, CALIFORNIA:
King Eider, *Somateria spectabilis*
Surf Scoters, *Melanitta perspicillata*
Black-throated Green Warbler, *Dendroica virens*
Solitary Vireo, *Vireo solitarius*
American Goldfinch, *Spinus tristis*
Lesser Goldfinch, *Spinus psaltria*
Song Sparrow, *Melospiza georgiana*
Common Moorhen (Gallinule), *Gallinula chloropsus*
Belted Kingfisher, *Megaceryle alcyon*
Anna's Hummingbird, *Calypte anna*
Ruby-crowned Kinglets, *Regulus calendula*

ORANGE COUNTY, CALIFORNIA:
Thick-billed Kingbird, *Tyrannus crassirostris*

18.
Weather and Nesting Conditions: The Christmas Island Story.

It is June of 1982. Ralph and Elizabeth Schreiber are virtually astride the equator and just east of the International Date Line. Dr. Schreiber is Curator of Ornithology at the Los Angeles County Museum of Natural History, and Elizabeth is his full-time unpaid assistant.

A mean elevation of three feet separates them from the vast encircling Pacific Ocean. It is flat, windy, humid, and hot—often 105°F.—but the activity and excitement more than compensate for all that. They are here amid the many colonies of unlimited numbers of seabirds, birds into the millions, to conduct a nesting survey on this largest coral atoll in the world, Christmas Island, twelve hundred miles south of Hawaii.

The "nursery" colonies involve five species of petrels and shear-waters, six species of tropicbirds, boobies and frigatebirds, and seven species of terns. The population of Wedge-tailed Shearwaters alone is a million and a half, of Sooty Terns, fourteen million!

It is noisy. The Sooty Tern colonies are the noisiest—and they are the most numerous species on the land—for they locate each other by calling, constantly. The colonies of frigatebirds and boobies are the least noisy, the loudest sounds they emit being the clattering of bills, and that primarily during courtship only. Unlike the sickening odor of moist guano that pervades some island nesting colonies off the coast of South America, the smell here is pleasant enough, for the island is baked under direct sunlight and clean winds freshen the air daily.

The seabird nesters on Christmas include Phoenix Petrels and White-throated Storm-Petrels; Wedge-tailed, Christmas, and Audubon's (a distinct minority) Shearwaters; Red-tailed Tropicbirds; Brown, Blue-faced, and Red-faced Boobies; Great and Lesser Frigatebirds; Blue-gray, Brown, and Black Noddies, and Sooty, Gray-backed, Crested, and White (Fairy) Terns. Most spend their lives airborne, floating on air currents, swooping down to feed on fish and squid in the ocean, and come to land only to nest. Many of these are burrow nesters.

Nests are marked by these researchers; both adult and young birds are banded; and there is a great deal of note-taking concerned with the dramatic but normal interactions of these birds as they are involved in courting, in territorial battles, in nest-building, in egg-laying, and in the hatching and fledging of the young; logs are carefully kept on the comings and goings of both parents as they feed and help their offspring slowly reach maturity. Slowly because, unlike most birds we are familiar with, some of these marine birds have a nestling time of at least four months, followed by a dependency on the parents of fourteen months. But not to worry; nesting is going well.

In a room in the Captain Cook Hotel, the alarm clock rings at 4:30 each morning. Hat, swim wear and tennis shoes. The rented pickup truck is loaded in the moist, warm darkness, and Ralph and Elizabeth start the journey to the colony they will study today. Dedicated ornithologists, they regard studying the birds here as the most interesting part of their work.

"It is very exciting working on the island; there are so many birds, and there is so much going on all the time. It is fascinating!" says Elizabeth. "And," adds Ralph, "it is such a pleasure just to be away from the telephone!"

The only road snakes a little more than halfway around the outer edge of but one side of the island. The rest of the way is driven by gosh and by feel over dirt or coral "meanderings" twisting between the many little lagoons. And though it is easy to get lost, and easier still for the pickup to fall through the hardpan surface—and this has happened to them—thanks to Ralph's intimate knowledge of the island and the location of each bird colony, they each day manage to get there and back.

A mechanical failure in the field could result in a very, very long walk, for there may not be another car along ever. Twice they have been caught out in the boonies with a flat tire and no spare. Because the few "towns" are far apart and distant from the nesting colonies— there are "Poland" and "London," two of the oldest, and "Banana," the newest (alas, "Paris" is now abandoned), each "town" being close to a coconut plantation—they drove back to the hotel on three tires and a wheel rim. Noisy and slow, but not much more uncomfortable than riding on four tires, they relate.

To evade the sweltering heat the Schreibers do much of their work before or after daylight, using head lanterns. In darkness the birds are especially easy to approach and handle for weighing, measuring and banding; and the nests can be more easily marked and the eggs counted. Most daylight hours are spent studying and recording bird behavior. It is never dull. By ten o'clock the team is usually headed back to breakfast and shelter.

𝒥

Returning to Christmas Island in November of 1982, the Schreibers are immediately aware that something is amiss. Hurrying out to the nesting colonies, they discover disappearance and devastation. In Ralph's words, "We discovered virtually a total reproductive failure on the island; the bird populations had essentially disappeared, and many dead and starving nestlings were present." An entire generation of seabird young had been obliterated. The nests were gone without a trace. A few skeletal remains were scattered about; most had been dragged off by the island's vast crab population. No such massive reproductive failure has ever been recorded in a tropical oceanic island.

Initially there were pangs of frustration that months of hard work done during previous visits were now down the tubes. That work was done in vain; it is all gone. Then there was exasperation upon learning that the local inhabitants were not even aware that the birds were gone or that anything was different. Elizabeth says quietly, "If there were only one person you could call and ask, 'How is the nesting going!'" And finally, after the overwhelming impact of the loss of so many birds, there remained the questions: Where have the adults gone? Have they survived? Will they return in normal numbers next year? Will they have a normal nesting?

The winter of 1982 and into the spring of 1983 there were many strange and unusual weather problems around the world, among them the worst drought on record in Australia, resulting in devastating brush fires, while at the same time unseasonally torrential rains flooded Ecuador and coastal Peru, and heavy rains combined with leviathan tides resulted in the worst winter destruction the California coast had seen in fifty years. All of these events have taken a toll on birds, especially seabirds.

By some it is blamed on an "El Niño," a massive climate upheaval that occurs every two to ten years around yuletide (which is why it is named "The Child"). The El Niño of 1982 may have been the worst in the past one hundred years. An El Niño occurs when the trade winds slow—and in 1982 they never even materialized—causing winds from the west to pick up, triggering in the Pacific a massive internal wave known as a Kelvin Wave. Warm water from the west sloshes thousands of miles back toward the coast of South America, and in time moves north along the coast of North America as well. The layer of warm water prevents the normal upwelling of cold nutrient-rich waters along the coast, which affects marine life from the phytoplankton base of the food chain on up. In the delicately interwoven warp and woof of winds, ocean currents, and water temperatures, the slightest variation may result in the dramatic disappearance from an area of entire populations of fish—and consequently the birds that feed on them.

The Schreibers believe this is what happened on Christmas Island, that the adults were forced to abandon the nestlings. They say that in such long-lived species, with life spans of twenty to thirty-five years, it is, according to ecological theory, normal evolutionarily for the adults to save themselves for later breeding when the food situation is improved.

But this is more than a story about the peccadilloes of life and death at the equator. When the hot water ran into Ecuador—smack on the equator, of course—it was funneled south along Peru and north along the coasts of Central America, Mexico, and at least as far as northern California, with drastic effects.

In June of 1983 an alarm was heard from Burr Henneman of the Point Reyes Bird Observatory: "The mating of hundreds of thousands of seabirds on the Farallon Islands (west of San Francisco) has been dramatically curtailed." A similar alarm has been heard from the Galápagos Islands. And from Chancay, Peru, Sister Cyrilla Evans writes also in June of 1983: "In the past month alone we have seen the carcasses of four seals and literally thousands of seabirds littering the rocky points and beaches of our particular area. It is a case of mass starvation, it appears, as the anchovies have sought colder waters. The fishing industry is in a state of bankruptcy...."

Is it simply a matter of isobars and tides? With funding from the National Science Foundation and the National Geographic Society the Schreibers were eager to return in summer-fall 1983 to learn when and if the birds returned, what reproductive cycles were reestablished, and what the birds' diet and reproductive success would be during recovery—if there was recovery.

This will be an ongoing saga for several years, as reports filter in from remote areas around the world. It is, of course, global. And while it is suspected that dramatic oceanic/atmospheric changes have affected seabird nesting many times in the history of the world, there is little question now but that 1982 produced the most severe Southern Oscillation or El Niño condition of the century. Why isn't there more certainty? Because, unfortunately, the recording and collating of accurate and comprehensive oceanographic data is limited to only the past ten years.

$\mathscr{I}$

A hurried thirty-hour visit by Elizabeth to Christmas in early May of 1983 found only the inshore-feeding Black Noddies breeding, some tropicbirds courting in the air, and, due to exceptionally heavy rains, even more flooding than had been evident in November 1982.

Then the long-awaited return by Ralph and Elizabeth on June 25, 1983, when a ten-day careful investigation revealed that "although some individuals of most species of birds have returned to the island, except for three species populations remain extremely low; only Black Noddy Terns, Crested Terns, and Lesser Frigatebirds are presently breeding in numbers that approach the island populations prior to the fall of 1982, when massive abandonment of island by adults of all species occurred."

ℐ

Dr. Schreiber's most recent trip to Christmas Island was in February 1984. He reports: "The recovery of the seabirds from the El Niño conditions is progressing normally. The few adults present are nesting successfully if they have formed pair bonds and food seems available for these few individuals."

A detailed study of his report shows that most birds are present in only fractions of their previous populations, although Schreiber predicts "as the food supply increases populations will increase."

This is a rare chance for ornithologists to study first-hand Nature's way of implementing seabird population control. The fittest survive. Thus, what is a catastrophe to birdwatchers, is an exciting opportunity to scientists.

Conditions in the Central Pacific are moving back towards normal. For both scientists and birdwatchers alike it is all very interesting and we end up back in Biology 1A pondering the old question: "What is normal?"

19.
Birding by the Numbers.

THE SIX RAIL DAY AT NEWPORT

January 28, 1983. While football fans eagerly await Super Bowl XVII in Pasadena, in the heart of Los Angeles the Emergency Operations Center has been activated and members of all departments are on standby alert. There have been numerous landslides, and flooded streets are plaguing the city. The Santa Monica Pier has been severely damaged, the Seal Beach Pier has been pulverized, the Pacific Ocean is smashing our coastline and sucking the bits and pieces out to sea.

The third major storm of the season has just passed through, southern California has already had more than twice its normal amount of rain, and yet another Arctic storm is coming fast, pushing twelve to fifteen foot waves before it. Compounding the danger, there will be a 7.1-foot tide at 8:11 A.M. Beach dwellers pray and fill sandbags.

And at such a time where would a devout birder be?

At Upper Newport Bay, of course, on the Orange County coast, where the flooded spartina grass, cattails and cordgrass may permit us to see several species of rails, including, if lucky, the very private Black Rail, so tiny it is an inch shorter than a Song Sparrow!

165

I was to have been joined by two birders, but the night before, after viewing the dismal weather reports on television, they had chickened out. So I call my Israeli friend, Jacob Szabo, hard at work on his doctoral dissertation in nuclear engineering, who will never say no—unless it is on a Saturday.

Considering all the roadblocks and washed-out highways, the big question is: Can we reach our destination at all? Once near the area we can, if necessary, park the car and wade in. This combination of an extremely high tide and huge ocean swells with the water already dumped into the estuary by the rainstorms makes it the most opportune time in the past forty years to see all the rails at Newport!

At 5:30 A.M. we leave home in rain-lashed darkness. Traffic southbound on the San Diego Freeway is light, however, and avoiding several roadblocks we make our way to Pacific Coast Highway. At 7:00 A.M. we enter Back Bay Drive from the ocean side, along the Newporter Inn, and it is not blocked off, at least not at this end. And the rain has ceased.

A short distance up the road we stop to bird, and positioned on the high bank, we scrutinize the edge of this tidal marsh, one of the last six or so remaining in all of southern California. It is daybreak but the lighting from the sun merely serves as a backdrop for a dramatic roiling cloud silhouette, black mushroom figures rising slowly to meet long black cloud fingers that drip down through the chill, wet, blue-gray air.

The silence is shattered by the alarm of a Marsh Wren that sputters and fumes, swelling its clean white breast and twitching a nervous tail over its rusty back. A Sora whinnies, and suddenly, almost subliminally, across the tops of the high marsh grass there is a bit of yellow (the bill), a dash of black (the body), and a speck of white (undertail coverts) as it melts into the grass and disappears. In Morse Code it was the letter "F" ($\cdot\cdot-\cdot$). That fast. With all this rain and our tidal problems I wonder if this Sora isn't sorry it didn't winter in Trinidad!

We drive on, birding as we go, and by 7:30 are at the cable crossing where most Black Rails have been sighted over the years crossing the road at extreme high tides. And here we meet other hard-core birders anticipating the appearance of the Black Rail. They are Arnold Small, active world birder, expert bird photographer, who has been an *American Birds* regional editor, as well as president of the American Birding Association and the Los Angeles Audubon Society; Jim Halferty, with whom in 1978 I birded across a good bit of Alaska; Shum Suffell with whom I shared my first sighting of Eared Trogon in Arizona, and whose "Birds of the Season" column I followed religiously in *Western Tanager* for well over fifteen years; and Hal Baxter who took over the writing of the column (along with Kimball Garrett) after Shum's recent death, and who called my attention to my first Chestnut-sided Warbler.

By 8:00 and with the extremely high tide, my Sora count is up to eight, some from very good looks from the high banks down onto the open feeding area below us. But this is Black Rail time!

Arnold and I are the only ones with rubber boots. I wade out to a point of land about twenty-five feet into the marsh so I may look toward the west away from any glare and down into an expansive cluster of mixed wild shrubbery and marsh plantings jutting out from the bank. This shoreline fringes broad stands of salicornia, spartina, cattails and cordgrasses; a climb up into this tangle to avoid the rising waters would be less exhausting and less public than flight to the steep hillside across the road. (This is bird brain thinking, of course.)

Jacob, wearing an old pair of street shoes, splashes right in and follows me, but then changes his mind and returns to the road and finally joins Arnold who stands facing me, but lower, looking into an opening in the same growth I concentrate on. The rest are closer to the road edge looking straight out into the same area.

Behind me, out on the water, I see Shovelers and Eared Grebes in profusion, as well as rafts of American Coots, each bird showing a chocolate drop on a white frontal plate. This is my second rail of the day. Yes, the same family!

Very dark Song Sparrows flit about, disturbed and scolding. Against the backdrop of snow-capped mountains to the east the sky is filled with gulls—Ring-bills, Californias and Bonaparte's—their white breasts glistening like snowflakes in the welcome sun. I think, "It's snowing gulls!"

Seemingly the tide is still rising. In the lagoon are Green-winged and Cinnamon Teal and apparently two different races of Savannah Sparrows—the Belding's, very dark, with much more streaking down the breast than the lighter *nevadensis*. Wigeon dabble in the shallows, and toward the far shore I watch several Great Blue Herons hunting, as we are, by remaining silent and unmoving and staring at where the prey should appear.

At 8:20, looking deep into the brushy tangle, I lock onto movement. It is the very tiny black-billed Black Rail! (This western race, *Laterallus jamicensis coturniculus*, is even smaller and darker than the nominate eastern subspecies *L.j. jamaicensis*.)

It moves toward the party near the road, then turns right and feeds its way slowly but wraith-like toward Arnold and Jacob, always under the canopy of the protective plants...now a bird, now a shadow, again a bird and instantly again a tiny part of the canopy shadow. From what I attribute to the excitement and force of habit, I hiss, "Black Rail going toward you, Arnold!"

Arnold, a very quiet birder, calmly answers that he has been watching it and cautions against talking. The Black Rail has already dissolved into the shadows. Jacob, patiently waiting in sopping wet shoes directly beside Arnold, misses the bird, as do the others closer to the road. My luck was the advantage of height. Later Jacob tells me that when "Arnold mumbled something about, 'There's Junior,' I thought he meant the Sora!" The gist of Arnold's message had evaporated as surely as had the Black Rail.

At 8:25 we all see in the same tangle of stalks and shrubs a Virginia and then a Clapper Rail. This Clapper at Newport is of the endangered Light-footed race, *Rallus longirostris levipes*. It is very richly colored, much like the eastern King Rail. It walks slowly across an open area as it feeds, apparently more hungry than wary. The Virginia is basically a pint-sized *levipes* race Clapper. Before departing we see several of each, but not the Black Rail again.

The sun is lost in the now-threatening clouds, but Arnold and I have seen five members of the Rail Family at Upper Newport. An hour later, in Central Park, Jacob and I are welcomed to the pond by a Common Moorhen (formerly Common Gallinule), its red frontal shield highly visible, another member of the Family *Rallidae*.

Six rails in a single day! But for me the third rail was, naturally, the most electrifying.

THE SIX-LEGGED HUMMINGBIRD

In Spring 1982 from South Texas came a report of a Rufous-crested

Coquette, a Mexican species of hummingbird. It touched off a veritable stampede of birdwatchers that was stemmed only when it was finally determined to be a *Selasphorous* hummingbird (probably either Allen's or Rufous). And it was understandable.

About two years before that, however, from the same area was reported a female Black-crested Coquette. It was the first record for the continent north of Mexico and birders flocked to the feeder it was visiting and confirmed the sighting of a species rare even in Mexico! Indeed, it had a white bar across the brown and golden-bronze lower back.

Finally came the day when the expert showed up. After but a short study session he announced it a Sphynx Moth! "Next time," he admonished the dismayed birders, "count the legs!"

BIG BEAR, BALDWIN AND A BAKER'S DOZEN OF SPARROWS

We meet at Big Bear dam, then caravan around the north side of the lake, making a left turn onto Shay Road and continue on around so we are at the west side of Lake Baldwin. July 10, 1983. With Kimball Garrett leading a Los Angeles Audubon Society field trip to Big Bear we first bird around Baldwin Lake. The lakes are close neighbors.

Piling out of the cars we hear the mewing, much like the eastern Catbird, of a Green-tailed Towhee. All binoculars focus on the shrub from which the noise emanates, and finally the bird hops up and poses, showing its adult red cap, green back and long green tail. Its white throat is bordered by a black whisker on either side. Peeking at us from the same bush is a juvenile with brown cap and back, and brown on the edge of its white throat, dark streaks mark the breast so it appears to be wearing a beard!

Baldwin Lake intermittently hosts (not in the dry years) the second largest breeding population of Eared Grebes in southern California. We watch and listen to their *Kweez! Kweez!* calling. The Pied-billed Grebes make a hooting call.

Scopes are brought out to study the Ruddy Ducks, Redheads, Ring-necks, Gadwalls and Cinnamon Teal. Flaunting their black wing tips, a flock of Avocets flies over. And across the road in the trees on the hillside we hear and see Mountain Chickadees—*Dee-dee-dee*—and an Ash-throated Flycatcher. Far across a field, obviously watching the birdwatchers from a tree, is an immature Cooper's Hawk showing its very long tail and clear belly (as contrasted to the underparts of Sharp-shinned Hawks on which the breast markings are extended down to include the belly). We stare at each other, only he doesn't need a scope.

Not widely known among birders, this piece of California is noted for more than its breeding Eared Grebes. If one goes a-lookin' on a day in July such as this, you can tote up thirteen different species of sparrows! Compared to some of the other passerines, most bird-watchers seem to feel that sparrows are nothing to get excited about. Ordinarily they are just part of the background, treated like the dancers in the back row of a chorus line. They may lack the pizzaz of warblers and the color of tanagers, but, I assure you, given some study they are a fascinating family, well worth looking into.

In the grasses very close to the lake we find Savannahs, with their streaked breasts and easily-spotted yellowish eyebrows. Savannahs, if their feathers are properly arranged, will show a breast spot (and this applies to every race of the species), a mark we see now and will see on five different species of the thirteen local sparrows. So much for the so-called identifying mark of the Song Sparrow.

In the grayish, pungent sagebrush just behind the shore grasses, we find the large Vesper Sparrow, also with streaking down the breast but much sparser than on the Savvies, and with white outer tail feathers. They also have noticeable cheek patches and distinct white eye rings and are, overall, paler than the main race of Savannahs, particularly in the widespread race of Vesper, *P. g. confinis*. Here also are Brewer's, the palest, smallest and slimmest of all the local sparrows. Vesper and Brewer's are local breeders in southern California and this is indeed one of the only localities for breeding Vesper Sparrows.

A wave of binoculars rises in unison to view the Common Night-hawk crying *Peent!* overhead. Because the outermost wing feather is the longest, its wings look more pointed than the wings of the Lesser Nighthawk. Its wings appear more rounded because the second wing feather is longer than the outermost one. These birds are fast flyers so you must be prepared to study this feature.

In a field two or three miles back from the lake toward Arrastre Creek, our ultimate destination, we find, again with white outer tail feathers and breast spot, the very "cheeky" chestnut-headed Lark Sparrows. And here also are Western Bluebirds calling my name—

Chuck-Chuck!—and also the larger and longer-winged Mountain Bluebirds calling their ethereal *Ve-e-e-r!* These open fields are typical for the Mountain Bluebirds; the Westerns, which prefer forests for their nesting, are in the fields now with their newly-fledged, speckly brown-breasted young.

Back in the grasses of the flatter meadows between the hills we find the large sooty-backed Sage Sparrows, marked on the head in dark gray and white and also bearing the dark "stickpin" on the breast. Flying away from us the black tail contrasts sharply with the rest of the plumage. Distinctive, too, is the expressive tail. As Kimball points out, "They wag their tails like crazy!" Often they run along the ground wagging their tails, much as would a thrasher. Interestingly, Sage and Brewer's Sparrows, it seems, are usually found singly; the Savvies, on the other hand, seem to appear in flocks.

Via an unmarked dirt road, we arrive at Arrastre Creek to search for a pair of reported Hepatic Tanagers. In the willows we find a single Anna's and an adult male Allen's Hummingbird; the latter species is a migrant, in fact, one of the earliest fall migrants in the state. (Their migration is well underway by late June.) Then on a hillside, feeding in the scarlet Indian paintbrush, a Calliope Hummingbird, and in flight from creekbed to bank, two Black-chinned Sparrows and a Dark-eyed (Oregon) Junco, our sixth and seventh sparrows of the day. The junco is a member of the sparrow family, after all!

Retracing our route back to Baldwin Lake we stop and find a Gray Flycatcher. Contrary to all other *Empidonax* flycatchers, which flick their tail up and then down, this species dips its tail periodically, and this is a good behavioral characteristic which helps to identify it. Then Kimball leads us to an area known since the turn of the century as the only colony of Cliff Swallows that nests in trees! Perhaps three hundred birds flutter about, feeding young in their mud nests plastered against the trunks of Ponderosa pines.

Along the south side of Big Bear Lake, we go east on Big Bear Boulevard and turn right at the "Campground" sign at Tulip Road to picnic at the foot of Forest Service Route 2N10 in Aspen Glen. After lunch we continue up 2N10 approximately two miles where there is a meadow on either side of the roadway. Kimball calls this unmarked spot "Metcalf Meadow."

Here we find *stephensi*, the gray-headed and the largest billed race of the Fox Sparrow, and again marked with a breast spot. It is singing from the broad swaths of ceanothus on the hillsides. In the wetter parts of the meadow, Lincoln Sparrows astride the corn lillies operatically sing a clear long note that plummets perhaps three tones downscale to a longer trilled note. And there are the noisy, nervous Song Sparrows and several Chipping Sparrows, rusty-capped, and emitting their high-pitched trilling, while Orange-crowned and Wilson's Warblers periodically "rise to the surface" along the wide swath of dense willows in splendid seclusion.

Those of us who go on over the drier desert slopes to the north easily find the Black-throated Sparrow, and locally high up on Mount San Gorgonio we find the nesting black-lored montane race of the White-crowned Sparrow, *Z. l. oriantha*, our twelfth and thirteenth species of sparrows for the day!

But the find of the day is our discovery of a pair of Williamson's Sapsuckers, the "odd couple," he black and white with dramatic white markings on his black head and red-throated, and she with whitish stripes and speckling over a brown body—the only color parts they share are their yellow bellies under black breasts. They use different approaches in carrying food to young in the nest hole, surprisingly not more than two feet above the ground. She flies in low from the back of the tree, he often flies to a good outpost where he can view us from a third of the way up the trunk of the tree and then "hitches" his way down the trunk backwards to reach the nest hole.

In the meadows are Western Wood-Pewee and Townsend's Solitaire calling its single bell-like note, and a Band-tailed Pigeon "fly-over," not unexpected up here. We watch for a time as Red-breasted Sapsuckers feed their nestlings in a hollow stump nest.

And as we meander under the trees near the stream towards the cars, we hear, *What peeves you?* Looking up we find the source of this concern, an Olive-sided Flycatcher.

In "Bird" I whistle back my own answer, "Nothing. It's been delightful, thank you!"

I'm sure he understood because he didn't ask again.

BIRD LOG

NOTE: *The following birds were spotted by Mr. Bernstein on the birding trip(s) described in this chapter. They are in the order they were sighted.*

NEWPORT BAY, CALIFORNIA:
Marsh Wren, *Cistothorus palustris*
Sora, *Porzana carolina*
Shoveler, *Spatula clypeata*
Eared Grebe, *Podiceps caspicus*
American Coot, *Fulica americana*
Song Sparrow, *Melospiza melodia*
Ring-billed Gull, *Larus delawarensis*
California Gull, *Larus californicus*
Bonaparte's Gull, *Larus philadelphia*
Green-winged Teal, *Anas carolinensis*
Cinnamon Teal, *Anas crecca*
Savannah Sparrow, *Passerculus sandwichensis*
American Widgeon, *Mareca americana*
Great Blue Heron, *Ardea herodias*
Black Rail, *Laterallus jamaicensis*
Virginia Rail, *Rallus limicola*
Clapper Rail, *Rallus longirostris*
Common Moorhen, (Gallinule), *Gallinula chloropus*

BIG BEAR LAKE, CALIFORNIA:
Fox Sparrow, *Passerella iliaca*
Lincoln Sparrow, *Melospiza lincolnii*
Song Sparrow, *Melospiza melodia*
Chipping Sparrow, *Spizella passerina*
Orange-crowned Warbler, *Vermivora celata*
Wilson's Warbler, *Wilsonia pusilla*
Black-throated Sparrow, *Amphispiza bilineata*
White-crowned Sparrow, *Zonotrichia leucophrys*
Williamson's Sapsuckers, *Sphyrapicus thyroideus*
Western Wood-Pewee, *Contopus sordidulus*
Townsend's Solitaire, *Myadestes townsendi*
Band-tailed Pigeon, *Columba fasciata*
Red-breasted Sapsucker, *Sphyrapicus varius*
Olive-sided Flycatcher, *Nuttallornis borealis*

BALDWIN LAKE, CALIFORNIA:
Green-tailed Towhee, *Chlorura chlorura*
Eared Grebe, *Podiceps caspicus*
Pied-billed Grebe, *Podilymbus podiceps*
Ruddy Duck, *Oxyura jamaicensis*
Redhead, *Aythya americana*
Ring-necked Duck, *Aythya collaris*
Gadwall, *Anas strepera*
Cinnamon Teal, *Anas cyanoptera*
Avocet, *Recurvirostra americana*
Mountain Chickadee, *Parus gambeli*
Ash-throated Flycatcher, *Myiarchus cinerascens,*
Cooper's Hawk, *Accipiter cooperii*
Savannah Sparrow, *Passerculus sandwichensis*
Vesper Sparrow, *Pooecetes gramineus*
Brewer's Sparrow, *Spizella breweri*
Common Nighthawk, *Chordeiles minor*
Lark Sparrow, *Chondestes grammacus*
Western Bluebird, *Sialia mexicana*
Mountain Bluebird, *Sialia currucoides*
Sage Sparrow, *Amphispiza belli*
Anna's Hummingbird, *Claypte anna*
Allen's Hummingbird, *Selasphorus sasin*
Calliope Hummingbird, *Stellula calliope*
Black-chinned Sparrow, *Spizella atrogularis*
Dark-eyed (Oregon) Junco, *Junco hyemalis oreganus*
Gray Flycatcher, *Empidonax wrightii*
Cliff Swallow, *Petrochelidon pyrrhonota*

20.
Birding at its Best.

March 10, 1983. It starts in cold and darkness at 2:00 A.M., and as the blushing sun rises to warm the desert earth, piece by piece it unfolds like the opening of a rare blossom into a memorable day of birding.

This last day of Canadian naturalist Alan Wormington's visit to southern California before his return to Point Pelee, Ontario, we are going on our final winter trip to the Salton Sea, perhaps to find the Olivaceous Cormorant reported there. Alan is the one asleep in the back seat. I keep our driver, Jon Dunn, awake with spirited discussion. At 3:45 we pick up Eugene Cardiff at the San Bernardino Museum, where he is curator of natural history. Alan awakes to make room for him, and we are off in Jon's little yellow car entertained by a growing tide of conversation, at times all four talking at once—of birds and birding:

Of the nest site last year of a pair of Zone-tailed Hawks on Santa Rosa Mountain just north of the sea and the Zone-tailed that spent the winter in the hills above Oceanside. Should the nesters return it will be at the end of April....The most common gulls at the sea in winter, according to Jon, are, in order: Ring-billed, Herring, California, Thayer's, Bonaparte's and Yellow-footed. And toss in a few Mew. In spring and fall add Franklin's and in summer the Laughing....A nice residential section in Brawley is the best place to find wintering (and, probably later, nesting) Costa's Hummingbirds. We will make a stop there, but Jon cautions that last year a neighborhood lady admonished him for walking through the alley with binoculars and told him he was lucky he wasn't shot! We will be cautious.

At 5:30 A.M. we are at the northwest corner of the sea. Silhouetted across the rippling mirror to our left are layers beyond layers of mountains receding into the red glowing horizon. Nearer, the sea surface and the lines of date palms are splashed with the crimson and purple of daybreak. In just a few minutes we stop in Brawley for breakfast and more good talk.

Gene tells of birding Harbor Dry Lake near Barstow where at certain times of the year he easily gets Short-eared Owls and Mountain Plovers. (It is new to me; I must try it!)....Alan recalls the birdwatcher I know from West Virginia who last year returned from Point Pelee with the astounding news that she had seen a possible Western Flycatcher there. He says it was later identified by its call as a Yellow-bellied Flycatcher!...Separating male from female first-year Red Crossbills is often difficult. Jon, who religiously keeps up with the literature, says, "If it's all red it's a male; otherwise, if the throat is yellow it's a male; if gray-throated, a female." What he is saying is: If unsure, go for the throat!

Seeking a life bird for Alan, we cruise slowly through Brawley. Ahead of us on a telephone wire, there it is, flaring its dark gorgette, a male Costa's Hummingbird! And another! Then, a Gila Woodpecker! Gene says though once common in this desert they are reduced in numbers and even on the Colorado River, though still fairly common, they are less numerous. Then there are two—a pair of Gila Wood-peckers!

Walking through the alleys we are flanked on either side by exotic subtropical plantings in backyards. The dramatic contrast with the scrubby low desert around us is striking. This lush and colorful oasis attracts many birds, and the Gila Woodpeckers have many palm trees available for nesting. We know of no birder who lives here, but marvel at the year list such a birder might compile! Here are Verdin and a Warbling Vireo. Cedar Waxwings fly over. Jon points out the house of the lady who chastised him and swears she ended her tirade by suggesting, "Why don't you go out to the country, where the birds are!"

The golf course at Del Rio Country Club produces our first of several pairs of Great-tailed Grackles of the day. A Northern Rough-winged Swallow flies from its perch on a wire, and Jon reminds: "At nesting time only nesters are found singly or in pairs; the migrants move through in flocks." Here are Cattle Egrets and Northern Mockingbirds a-courting. We look for Mountain Plover, at Jon's suggestion, in the brown earthy fields. They may have all gone north by now. We find flocks of gulls: Ring-bills, pearly-backed, their fronts gleaming like starched white shirts in the warming sunlight; Californias, darker-backed with brown splotching down their vests. In the fields of salt bush and mesquite are more Verdin, and the Silky-Flycatcher—Phainopepla—one blue-black and one gray-brown, male and female, both red-eyed with crests upright as if abruptly startled. Gene says that Guy McCaskie, our *American Birds* regional editor, told him Phainopeplas do not nest here at the sea. Surely it could not be far. In the adjoining desert, perhaps? I seem to recall their nesting north of here in Morongo Valley.

At Finney Lake, east of the sea, we find Eared Grebes and Cinnamon Teal, and the tules are alive with honking and squawking Yellow-headed Blackbirds well into nest-building. Here a Cactus Wren; there the excitable Marsh Wrens; a Black-crowned Night-Heron, Common Gallinule, and the downscale whinny of the Sora. In the salt cedar is the *gambelii* race of the White-crowned Sparrow. (In full spring there will be a few of the *oriantha* race here with their black lores and bigger pink bills.) Then out from under the long skirts of a paloverde tree another life bird for Alan—the black-faced Abert's Towhee skitters to the nearest clump of foliage! Gene reminds us the most secretive birds may be those of the desert, which have very little cover. Double-crested Cormorants perch on snags in the lake, long wings stretched to dry.

While watching an Orange-crowned Warbler we listen to the liquid song of the House Wren, followed by the "irritation buzz" of a Bewick's Wren. And as I study the Bewick's, I once again confirm that the white on its tail is virtually useless as a mark. The white is spotted only on the outer webbing of the two outermost tail feathers, which makes it difficult to see because one doesn't often get to see the underside of this wren's tail, and dorsally these marks are normally covered by inner tail feathers.

At Morongo Valley, Verdins stayed through the winter, and a Vermilion Flycatcher wintered in nearby Calipatria. Gene knows. He makes the San Bernardino Bird Alert tapes. The recent heavy rains have hit this low desert valley hard. Bumping along courageously over rutted dirt "roads" that just last week were under water, we pass many acres of reviving sugar beets and barley....Alan thinks the new name Three-toed Woodpecker is a "disaster," that it will remain ambiguous, difficult to distinguish from the other three-toed woodpecker, now simply called Black-backed....So we get back to a previous change, from Audubon's to Yellow-rumped Warbler, which mark is shared by at least five warbler species!...We all agree more lumpings are in the offing, namely, Northwestern with American Crow, King with Clapper Rail, Glaucous-winged with Western Gull, and Iceland with Thayer's Gull....We spy two male Northern Harriers (once Marsh Hawks, remember?) and Jon says Kimball Garrett, now of the Los Angeles Natural History Museum, calls them "Northern Harassers!"

From the back seat of the moving car Alan finds us Mountain Plover in a field with green young plantings approximately six inches in height. "Brown earthy fields," indeed! Jon suffers our taunting with good humor. In the scopes we identify, feeding in separate flocks, some thirty-five Mountain and ten Black-bellied Plovers. In flight the Mountain Plovers have a clean white stripe on the secondaries and a dark rump; the Black-bellies' wing stripe is blurry gray and it shows the white rump. Getting a photograph of a Mountain Plover is all but impossible for Gene. The bird he wants, with white forehead, black crown, big black eye and buffy breast, consistently turns and toddles off in every other direction!

It is 10:00 A.M., and we are already peeled down to light sport shirts. Moving between the dirt dikes we study Burrowing Owls. A flock of Tree Swallows passes overhead—either wintering here or migrants. Certainly the Red-winged Blackbirds we see are single or paired and make no secret they nest locally! Here is a small blue-gray butterfly with white spots on the wings. Gene and Alan, both introduced to natural history and eventually to birds through butterfly-collecting in childhood, identify it as a Checkered Skipper.

At Red Hill Marina the dike is heavily covered with small dead fish, mostly skeletal now. They are *telepia*, Gene explains, brought in from tropical Africa to clean algae from the water. There are heavy die-offs each winter, not from the overabundance of salt, the first thing that comes to mind, but from the cold temperature of the water in winter! He assures us they breed like crazy each spring and are in no danger of extermination.

Here are many Great Blue Herons and a Great Egret, a fly-over White-faced Ibis alternately flapping and gliding, Black-necked Stilts, a lone Common Yellowthroat, and Herring, California, and Ring-billed gulls. And here, too, is a first-year Yellow-footed Gull! It is large, the size of a Western Gull, from which it was recently split off as a separate species, and is equally large-billed. On this standing bird the wing coverts are very gray over the dark brown wings. It has a black terminal band on the tail and black wing tips—and pinkish-tan legs and feet! Here also are two Mew Gulls, rare at the Salton Sea, showing a darker mantle than the Ring-bills with more white in the wing tips and thin dainty greenish bill and greenish legs.

Cliff Swallows noisily seem to be exchanging gossip as they gather mud balls to form into nests on the underside of an abandoned wooden bridge now marooned far out in the water. Snowy Egrets comb through the sea's shallows while the cumbersome red-billed Caspian and the quick, slender Forster's Terns hunt to and fro over the waters.

At 11:25 we are on a lonely dike surrounded by water on three sides. Here the New River enters the sea. I study the bill of a California Gull in breeding plumage—the black spot on the bill almost disappears, and the red spot gets redder! From the very end of the dirt extends a staggered line of dead trees in several feet of water. In the branches of each, several Double-crested Cormorants have built or are building nests. At eleven o'clock (directionwise) on one of the farthest trees out stands a smaller and slimmer cormorant. It has white edging around its gular pouch. The Olivaceous Cormorant! This is the fourth California record. A good bird for one's state list.

Scoping around on the sea we find battalions of White Pelicans fishing in unison, "by the numbers," and Canvasback, Shoveler, many Lesser and a pair of Greater Scaup. A Marbled Godwit flies over, flashing rufous in the wings.

> Gene, who has been very close to the Salton Sea's problems for most of his life, explains some of the present ones. A lawsuit has been brought by the San Bernardino Audubon Society against Union Oil to close down a geothermal plant which, it is alleged, operating as it is will salt the sea out of existence long before its time. He feels also the threat of killing the sea completely by oversalting from normal farm irrigation drainage would be circumvented by building a huge circular dike in the center of the sea. He points out this would also provide roosting and even nesting sites for birds.

At 12:15 P.M. we are at Unit I, close to the extreme south end, where we park and share lunch—someone brought sweet rolls, someone oranges, someone, most thoughtfully, water—and walk in, examining the ponds on either side of the dirt road as we go. A pair of Whimbrels! Jon says this is the earliest record for a spring migrant Whimbrel inland! Horned Larks overhead and Meadowlarks in full song on perches. The small, gray *saltonis* race of Song Sparrow.

"My heart goes where the wild goose goes"....Hundreds of Snow and Ross's Geese feed in the ponds, and we have plenty of time to study them. The smaller Ross's has a more rounded head and short red bill, as contrasted with the slope-headed, "black-lipped" Snow. Ross's immatures are much paler than the young Snows. In flight the Ross's shows a narrower wing and faster wing beat than does the Snow Goose.

Also in the ponds, feeding like dowitchers, but smaller, grayer and shorter-billed, are several Stilt Sandpipers, the white supercilium accentuated by the dark cheek patch. The south end of the Salton Sea is the only place they winter in California. Dainty Least Sandpipers are plentiful, as are Avocets, Long-billed Curlews, Green-winged Teal, Dunlin, Long-billed Dowitchers, Willets, and Lesser Yellowlegs; and a female Eurasian Wigeon is found by Gene! Common Snipe fly frightened from pond to pond.

At 1:50, having raced north, we are at Salton City, again on the west side of the sea. This is the best place for Yellow-footed Gulls, especially in summer. Several are here now, together with Glaucous-winged and the pigeon-headed Thayer's Gulls, both rare at the Salton Sea. The Yellow-footeds are first- and second-year birds, and it is easy to study them on the ground. As do all three-year gulls, the second-year bird looks much like the adult, with sooty-gray wings, but retains the black terminal tail band and a dark spot on the bill tip. Strange that for so many years this three-year gull was lumped with the four-year Western Gull! (This summer I will see the adult with the all-white tail and no black tip on the bill!)

There are Red-breasted Mergansers on the sea here. From this point years ago I saw my "California" Brown Booby. Alan points out a tiny Western Pygmy Blue, the smallest butterfly in North America! In the nearby ponds with the Long-billeds is a Short-billed Dowitcher, which John confirms is the earliest record for inland southern California! We flush the dowitchers so we may hear their calls. The Long-billed series of notes is higher pitched than the deeper, more mellow three-note call of the Short-billed. The key to telling them apart is not in the number of notes called but the pitch or tone. In other words, the key is the key they call in! And Jon stresses that, contrary to popular belief, there is no overlap in the calls.

Farther north we find Semipalmated Plover and a few Western Sandpipers, and still farther we are at the puddle, near which on April 27, 1974, a Curlew Sandpiper was seen for only the second time in southern California, a fourth record for the state! Having seen it then—it stayed around for twenty-four hours—both Jon and Gene check this area about this time every year, always hoping. Today there are Sanderlings and Snowy Plovers, but no Curlew Sandpiper.

At 5:10 P.M. we arrive back at the San Bernardino Museum. Gene Cardiff's workshop/playground/lab/study, his hobby, his full-time occupation, his home away from home. It is located between Loma

Linda and Redlands at the California Street offramp from I-10 (the San Bernardino Freeway), a new and modern building, and we are invited in to continue our birdwalk through Gene's bird collection.

Two hours pass like minutes as we revel in the displays, study the birds, and discuss problems of preparing and preserving both study skins and life mounts. It is unique among life mount collections, because Gene, a licensed and exceedingly circumspect collector, himself collected, mounted, and posed virtually every bird in every exhibit in the vast expanse of floor-to-ceiling glass casing—a comprehensive display of meticulously mounted western birds of land and sea. There are also glass cases holding actual nests and eggs, and ("Just push the button") the songs and calls of many! We are viewing what is really a one-man show painstakingly created over an entire lifetime—a work of art.

The personal secrets of birding lore, concern for the habitat, and the thrill of discovery have today been shared with good friends. And to each of us it is apparent that birding at its best has more elements to it than merely finding and identifying birds, and that this was indeed a memorable day, birding at its best!

BIRD LOG

NOTE: *The following birds were spotted by Mr. Bernstein on the birding trip(s) described in this chapter. They are in the order they were sighted.*

BRAWLEY, CALIFORNIA:

Costa's Hummingbird, *Calypte costae*
Gila Woodpecker, *Melanerpes uropygialis*
Verdin, *Auriparus flaviceps*
Warbling Vireo, *Vireo gilvus*
Cedar Waxwing, *Bombycilla cedrorum*
Great-tailed Grackle, *Quiscalus mexicanus*
Northern Rough-winged Swallow, *Stelgidopteryx serripennis*
Cattle Egret, *Bubulcus ibis*
Northern Mockingbird, *Mimus polyglottos*
Ringbilled Gull, *Larus delawarensis*
California Gull, *Larus californicus*
Verdin, *Auriparus flaviceps*
Phainopepla, *Phainopepla nitens*
Eared Grebe, *Podiceps nigricollis*
Cinnamon Teal, *Anas cyanoptera*
Yellow-headed Blackbird, *Xanthocephalus xanthocephalus*
Cactus Wren, *Campylorhynchus bunneicapillus*
Marsh Wren, *Cistothorus palustris*
Black-crowned Night-Heron *Nycticorax nycticorax*
Common Moorhen (Gallinule), *Gallinula chloropus*
Sora, *Porzana carolina*
White-crowned Sparrow, *Zonotrichia leucophrys gambelii*
Abert's Towhee, *Pipilo aberti 'i*
Double-crested Cormorant, *Phalacrocorax auritus*
Orange-crowned Warbler, *Vermivora celata*
House Wren, *Troglodytes aedon*
Bewick's Wren, *Thryomanes bewickii*

SALTON SEA, CALIFORNIA:

Mountain Plover, *Charadrius montanus,*
Black-bellied Plover, *Pluvialis squatarola*
Burrowing Owl, *Athene cunicularia*
Tree Swallow, *Tachycineta bicolor*
Red-winged Blackbird, *Agelaius phoeniceus*
Great Blue Heron, *Ardea herodias*
Great Egret, *Casmerodius albus*
White-faced Ibis, *Plegadis chihi*
Black-necked Stilt, *Himantopus mexicanus*
Common Yellowthroat, *Geothlypis trichas*
Herring Gull, *Larus argentatus*
California Gull, *Laruws californicus*
Ring-billed Gull, *Larus delawarensis*
Yellow-footed Gull, *Larus livens*
Mew Gull, *Larus canus*
Cliff Swallow, *Hirundo pyrrhonota*
Snowy Egret, *Egretta thula*
Caspian Tern, *Sterna caspia*
Forster's Tern, *Sterna forsteri*
Double-crested Cormorant, *Phalacrocorax auritus*
Olivaceous Cormorant, *Phalacrocorax olivaceus*
American White Pelican, *Pelecanus erythrorhynchos*
Canvasback, *Aythya valisineria*
Northern Shoveler, *Anas clypeata*
Lesser Scaup, *Aythya affinis*
Greater Scaup, *Aythya marila*
Marbled Godwit, *Limosa fedoa*
Whimbrel, *Numenius phaeopus*
Horned Lark, *Eremophila alpestris*
Western Meadowlark, *Sturnella neglecta*
Song Sparrow, *Melospiza melodia*
Snow Goose, *Chen caerulescens*
Ross's Goose, *Chen rossii*
Stilt Sandpiper, *Calidris himantopus*
Least Sandpiper, *Calidris minutilla*
American Avocet, *Recurvirostra americana*
Long-billed Curlew, *Numenius americanus*
Green-winged Teal, *Anas crecca*

Dunlin, *Calidris alpina*
Long-billed Dowitcher, *Limnodromus scolopaceus*
Willet, *Catoptrophorus semipalmatus*
Lesser Yellowlegs, *Tringa flavipes*
Eurasian Wigeon, *Anas penelope*
Common Snipe, *Gallinago gallinago*
Yellow-footed Gull, *Larus livens*
Glaucous-winged Gull, *Larus glaucescens*
Thayer's Gull, *Larus thayeri*
Red-breasted Merganser, *Mergus serrator*
Short-billed Dowitcher, *Limnodromus griseus*
Semipalmated Plover, *Charadrius semipalmatus*
Western Sandpiper, *Calidris mauri*
Sanderling, *Crocethia alba*
Snowy Plover, *Charadrius alexandrinus*
Loggerhead Shrike, *Lanius ludovicianus*
Red-shouldered Hawk, *Buteo lineatus*
Red-tailed Hawk, *Buteo jamaicensis*
Ferruginous Hawk, *Buteo regalis*

21.
Taking a Guided Bird Tour.

NO MATTER HOW GOOD the birding is in your own backyard, neighborhood, or state, perhaps it is time to surrender to the lure of adventure and take a tour of an entirely new and different area. All of us, whether listers or not, have certain birds not native to our own area that we'd especially like to see. A professional birding tour may supply the right mix of birds, adventure, and expertise.

There are locations even in our own country, let alone the whole North American continent, virtually impossible to get to without help. Once there, the sought-after bird may be impossible to find without a guide. And if one presumably made it to the "virtually-impossible-to-reach" site, one would either find no vehicle for rent or no road to drive on. In other cases to go it alone may indeed be possible but may be a waste of money, time, and energy. In countries outside our own the problems are magnified.

Given political realities, certain prime birding areas are much more easily birded through tour arrangements. These include countries such as Cuba, China, and Israel, as well as bits of land always under threat of being closed off for the sake of economy, such as Attu, that farflung island outpost which the Coast Guard may have to abandon.

185

To be part of a group that shares your interest in birdwatching, to make new birding friendships, to exchange information and know-how about birds and birdwatching, and to be at the elbow of a birding expert who not only identifies the birds but explains the how and why of identification—these are only some of the advantages of an organized birding tour. The agency sponsoring the trip will arrange safe and effective transportation, no matter the condition of the roads and no matter the weather; and it will make sure group members are adequately fed and securely housed.

Your tour leader, however, is not merely an arranger of logistics. He is an expert on the particular location being visited. He has eaten there and slept there and birded there previously, and he knows where to look for rarities and how to recognize them, much as you would know where to look for which birds in your own local park.

Assume you live in New Jersey and decide to see the birds of California for the first time. You can make the trip without special help and pick up many of the California specialties by merely wandering around; but if time and funds are important to you, signing on with a tour is economical and more bird-efficient, for in a fraction of the time you would otherwise spend, you will certainly view, without fatigue, a very high percentage of all California birds. Even if the cost were more than that of birding it alone, you would still be ahead eventually, because it would probably require at least two trips, plus many days of planning, conferring, map-studying, and driving, driving, driving to see the same number of species you would see easily on a California tour.

An itinerary planned by people who have been over the territory numerous times and who know and understand its hazards and its blessings is often well worth the price. As a tour member you leave arrangements to others and sit back and concentrate on the birds and the scenery and the informative discussions at dinner. Most birding tours on today's market are a bargain, so unless you get your kicks out of preparing and planning your own trip, including the driving and including finding your own birds—and I am somewhat that way myself—let the expert guide you.

Expense is never a guarantee of quality. Although the most expensive is not necessarily the best, you usually get what you pay for. On some of the "bargain" trips the leader's pay is often only the cost of the trip. You may find him more interested in helping himself find birds than in helping you. Wisdom dictates you should ask around and consult your friends as to which agency and which leaders are the best to go with.

Here are a few tips which may help you if you do join a professional tour at some time.

● Make the most of the first opportunity that arises to see a new, hard-to-find bird. You may not get another chance, so feel free to speak up loud and clear if you do not see the bird the rest of the group says it is seeing. The bird may never be found again on the entire trip—nor even, if it's very rare, on any other trip. Don't count on another chance.

● Anticipate not merely experiencing the birds unique to the area, but the culture as well, wherever you go. Of course, you should not expect American-style accommodations, food, or service in another country. They may be better, they may be worse, they may be neither, only different. In France, as a benefit of your birding tour, you should expect to experience French food and culture; in India, you should expect to be given the opportunity to sample Indian life. The world is not America, and you should expect new things. Even in our own country Patterson, New Jersey, is a far cry from Terlingua, Texas, and San Francisco very different, even in accommodations, from Patagonia, Arizona.

● Be prepared for arrangements that make the most of a location. If you are lucky, you may expect on a tour of the Big Bend region of Texas to be awakened before sunup and driven to a wild prairie where a campfire will be built for cooking breakfast and where you may watch the rosy sunrise, listening to the dawn chorus of Cassin's Kingbirds while sipping your morning coffee.

On a tour of the southwestern United States in months when it gets unbearably hot in the afternoons, you'll go off birding at first light, and the bulk of your birdwatching will be done before noon. After that it is time for lunch and siesta. Birding will recommence at about four o'clock when it is cool again. (This kind of schedule applies, of course, to most tours in the equatorial zone.)

In the far north of Alaska in the spring, when it is daylight for twenty-two hours every day, you may expect to bird for as long as you can keep your eyes open, although most newly arrived species are discovered in the morning sweeps and that is the most productive birding time. Then, when your body is weary from a long day of hiking and excitement, you will lie down to sleep. However, when some birding glutton throws open the door to your hut and roars, "Siberian Rubythroat on the north runway!" be prepared to pull on your boots and go.

In East Africa you should expect to spend at least a week in one of the luxurious government-owned lodges, where a waiter will wake you each morning with coffee, or tea, as you prefer, and where you may stay awake all night watching the animals come and go at the well-lit water hole nearby. You should expect also to spend at least one week in a tented camp, so that you may experience the real wilderness of the country by listening each night to the snorting scream of an elephant feeding just a few feet from your head behind the canvas of the tent wall, or the annoyed growling of awakened lions, or the heavy sounds of grunting and gasping as hippos munch the grass between the tent rows.

On an island-hopping tour in and around the Bay of Fundy in fall you should expect to be put up in boarding houses. There are very few motels. These private homes are warm, the beds are clean, and although the food is simple and most of it comes from the sea, I treasure memories of the well-stocked tables of the Northeast; and I must say that every home-cooked meal I have ever had there was delicious.

Progress has come, I understand, to Attu, that outermost piece of America at the very end of the Aleutian chain, where birders each year search for strays from Siberia, just forty miles away. Today the birders bicycle to the site of a good bird. In 1978, with no bikes, we walked or ran constantly. Today the housing there is also much improved—one still needs a sleeping bag but is assigned a bunk bed in a stove-warmed building. That's luxury!

• Be prepared to dress for local weather. Consult with your tour agency as to what clothing to take, but by all means, especially if you are headed north, take with you a substantial set of rain gear, preferably two-piece with a hood. For the south, including and especially Florida, though you may not need a jacket you almost certainly will need long-sleeved shirts, if only to keep the sun and the mosquitoes off your bare arms.

Footwear in Kenya is relatively unimportant, inasmuch as you will be chauffeured to each game preserve to view the birds and animals from an open-top Land-Rover or VW bus. The only walking you'll be doing will be at your campsite. The drivers are under orders, outside of particular areas and barring emergencies, not to allow tourists out of the vans.

In contrast, at Gambell, on St. Lawrence Island in the Bering Sea, the shore is composed of rounded rocks the size of walnuts which give way underfoot, making walking very difficult and energy-consuming, especially if you are hurrying to check out the report of a Ross's Gull on an ice floe out at the point. For both loose rock and the pillowy tundra of the North I have found most satisfactory a pair of knee-high rubber boots with felt liner inserts, boots large enough to accommodate an extra pair of wool socks.

Rely on layers of clothing as opposed to single, heavy, burdensome garments, so that as the weather changes you may accommodate to it by peeling or adding layers. Drip-dry is convenient and lets you travel light, rinsing out what needs rinsing each evening.

• Always carry a supply of insect repellent, inasmuch as there are many states in our country where ticks, chiggers and mosquitoes seem never to have had a decent meal until you arrive (among these, Texas is noteworthy). Another must is a good handful of Lomotil pills. Merely using ice cubes in your drink or partaking of a salad where the lettuce has been washed in the local water, whether in the Arctic Circle or south of the border, may make you glad you have Lomotil on hand.

• Most leaders of tours are there more for the pleasure of birding than for the money they make. And most of them, if you will but ask, may be delighted to bird before or after "the regular day." On a tour I took to the great Northeast—although "officially" the birding started each day after breakfast and ended at dinnertime—in company with the tour leader, I got in at least one hour of birding before breakfast and an hour or so after dinner. Often a guide is concerned that he is making it too long a day for tired tour members. But tour guides love to bird; that's why they are there.

Thanks to our guide, my first afternoon of birding Africa at Lake Naivasha in Kenya was one of the most exciting of my life. Arriving tour members, after the very long trip and a heavy lunch, went off to nap, paying up for their jet lag. But our guide invited anyone who wanted to go birding just to call her. I was knocking on her door before most of the others were reaching for their tea. We identified Black Crakes, Lilly-trotters, Lilac-breasted Rollers—more than seventy species of birds new to me in just two hours! And as are all good and professional guides, she was delighted and eager to bird with anyone interested in "her" birds.

● Prepare for your tour, if possible, by talking to birders who have visited the area, borrowing their checklists. Undoubtedly the tour agency itself will furnish an up-to-date checklist of birds, and you may determine which species to anticipate finding. Study field guides and books on the particular area, so that you have a fairly good idea of what you're looking for when you get there. Also, read all you can find about the area you will visit, so that you can enjoy discovering the people, partaking of the food and the way of life, and experiencing the geography and the climate on-site.

● Get yourself in good physical shape with walking and regular exercise. A leader slows his pace to conform to the slowest member at the expense of other members.

● Do be flexible. Although the itinerary says, "Lunch at noon at Pedro's world-famous Taco Hacienda," should a very unusual bird be discovered en route and an extra hour or so spent showing it to each person, don't demand your lunch at noon at Pedro's, for obviously you'll not arrive at the famous hacienda on time. Remember, the birds are not on a schedule, and they are rarely on time.

Where in the world you go will depend to a great extent on what country and which birds you want to see. In my earlier years I used to leaf through bird books, looking at pictures of exotic species, and there were many that were so absolutely out-of-this-world I doubted they really existed: I had to see them to believe them. The Saddle-bill Stork of Africa was such a bird for me, a fantasy, really a cartoon of a bird, something "made up." Then on my very last day in Africa I saw one, and it made a believer of me.

Of course, for you who resist joining any tours, going your own way alone even if it is only a wild goose chase—well, a wild goose chase is fun, too!

22.
A Long Look into the Future.

THIS IS December 23, 2020. We have gathered for the annual Christmas Bird Count at Malibu. In the old days we were separated into small groups and each met in an assigned area. No need for that now. We are going to count a mere dozen or so species, give or take a few. Since the 1980s more than four hundred species of birds have been removed from the *North American Checklist of Birds,* several thousand from our hemisphere.

We meet on a high hill in the Santa Monica Mountains just in front of Pepperdine University. With very little effort and greatly improved optics we can view land birds as well as any possible pelagics (we are always looking for alcids) virtually without moving. The new binoculars enable us to pick up a tiny storm petrel three miles out to sea; it shows up as large and clear as would an albatross at a hundred feet through 10x50s in days gone by. And the infrared switch turns night into bright daylight.

We rely, of course, on the buzzing of the computerized ultrasound/intervention/locater to alert us to action. The hand-held video screen pinpoints precisely where a bird may be perched or flying within a radius of three miles; its accuracy is based on echo-reflection. So we really don't have to move. And when we do, we fly off strapped into our jet flightpacks, like those developed for outer space in the '80s.

Oh, there are still problems. The few species of birds remaining—aside from the European Starling, House Finch and House Sparrow, the "three great adapters"—seem always to feed on the other side of the tree. That hasn't changed! The inventor who first produces X-ray binoculars, in full color, so birdwatchers can see through foliage and tree trunks, will be honored with nothing less than the Roger Tory Peterson Golden Wing of Distinction by our WHFOU (Western Hemisphere Field Ornithologists Union).

This is, of course, a different kind of birding than we enjoyed forty years ago. But this is a different world. Almost all species of avifauna have been extirpated. This is an empty world where we birdwatch mechanically, almost out of habit, desperately hoping to discover a single stray vestige of one of the species that has been adjudged extinct.

Today we can only read in wonder and amazement about "waders" and "peeps"—Oh, what I would give to see such a thing as a Golden-Plover!—and "gulls" and "gannets" and "boobies" and "terns" and "guillemots." The mere sound of these names is romantic! The world must have been a delightful place to live in then, filled with chips and calls and the songs of birds.

The buzzer sounds! Each birder on the count checks the locater index video screen. All binoculars—because we all are locked onto the master direction/elevation finder carried by our leader—focus in perfect unison on an orange tree to the southeast far down a canyon where once there was the quiet sanctuary of a seminary.

We are hushed. My heart beats faster. "There it is, a Greater Roadrunner!"

This is the only real excitement of the day. Counting the same few species all day long is dull business. This is the first roadrunner on the Malibu Count in at least three years! This species has undergone many name changes by the WHFOU, Committee on Nomenclature. It started with Medium Roadrunner because it was learned an even greater race existed in a small hamlet in Siberia, then it went from Lesser Roadrunner to Desert Roadrunner to Desert Runner to Desert Walker and by then—twenty-six years later—they discovered the Russians never had a roadrunner after all. It had all been a terrible mistake, due to a mislabeled study skin, so it ended up again as the Greater Roadrunner.

A few birders elect to fly across to inspect it with the naked eye. The rest of us watch our leader, Kimball Garrett (his former co-leader Jean Brandt retired last year) punch in the report on the group's computer which is connected directly with the Chief Christmas Count Computer in Laurel, Maryland. Oh, paperwork was done away with long ago!

Instantly we get back our position hemispherewide among all groups participating in the Christmas Count. In contrast to the 1983 count when one hundred sixty-five species were recorded (thirty-five thousand individual birds) when we were in thirty-second place nationwide, we have today spotted twelve species (ten thousand individuals) and are oddly enough in thirty-second place again, but this time hemispherewide.

We carefully protect the few bird species remaining now on earth. Why earlier watchers of birds did not succeed in doing likewise is, of course, complicated and quite baffling; we have been taught that to protect wildlife and preserve it for the generations that will come is one of the highest purposes of mankind. Birds can't speak for themselves, but in a civilized world they shouldn't have to.

We know a world without birds is an empty world. So who will speak for the birds?

What birds are still with us, aside from the "three great adapters?" They are the stay-at-homes, the resident nonmigratory species and the inland migrants that did not cross coastal borders. Those that strayed beyond the three-mile limit line along any coastline anywhere in the world met with immediate laser beam annihilation from satellite-based defense systems meant to intercept incoming nuclear missiles. Constant improvement over the decades gave us weaponry so sensitive it would automatically and immediately zap a hummingbird as surely and easily as small boys in knickers toting shotguns along the Sespe in the '20s and '30s "plinked" condors in California. A suspicious and wary world.

Long before our coastal defenses were in place the watched-for passerines, particularly wood warblers and flycatchers were sadly depleted because of clearcutting of forests in Central and South America. A bird reaching its wintering grounds during the '80s and

'90s was confronted with resident species competing for food and an almost total absence of habitat. The same thing happened in Southeast Asia. The few western birds that survived to fly north for nesting in springtime had to go farther and farther north to find forest habitat in North America. Forest acreage diminished dramatically as the result of air and water contamination and acid rain.

Birds of the prairie—the meadowlarks and pipits and longspurs and some species of sparrows—simply put, had no prairie to go to by the year 2000. As the forests were cut down they were quickly turned into farmland and powdered and sprayed with chemicals cumulative and ultimately deadly to wildlife.

Eventually the more "advanced" parts of North America changed to a more efficient and easier controlled method of farming called hydroponics. That helped man; it didn't help the birds. Farmlands were hastily converted; buildings and homes and highways and airports were constructed, rivers and streams were dammed and channelized and paved with cement. Wall-to-wall cities hardened into concrete.

The tidal marshes died as well. The buildup of toxicity from herbicides and insecticides at the seashore killed every living thing in, on and over the sand. Shorebirds died of starvation or toxic poisoning. Marshes were converted to marinas. There was no other use for them. Today only deep-sea fish survive, and no shellfish whatever.

All raptors are "very rare to extinct" in this year of 2020. They were at the top of the food chain, the terminal catchall for all toxic chemicals. Now, free from predation from the air, rodents have multiplied so it seems at times they are vying with man for control of the planet!

Finally, according to our history books, there was committed an avian genocide of sorts by an offshore oil industry that, despite guarantees to governments that it would not happen, leaked and spilled, leaked and spilled—all inadvertent—until offshore oil was no more. Great flocks of migrating birds met their end in oil slicks on ocean waters all over the world. Extinction by inadvertence?

With the passage of time it is obvious that the existence of wildlife, birds in particular, is being placed in jeopardy by some of the works of man. I have spent a goodly portion of my adult life, both by involvement with the Audubon Society and individually, devoted to the conservation of wildlife and its habitats. I believe, very simply, that wildlife in all its forms is as entitled as we are to live unmolested on this planet. There must always be an active conservation movement ready and willing to speak out on behalf of all those creatures that cannot speak out in their own defense. We should take seriously and personally man's obligation to insure the survival of all species.

I have two grandchildren, very young yet and all giggles and large wonder-filled eyes and occasional mock grownup attitudes. When we go for a "hike" and lose ourselves in unfamiliar parks or woods—which we do often—and I ask a question like, "Is this finally the path back to the car?" Matthew, seven, looks very serious and says, "I think so." Hillary, four, purses her lips and says, "I know so!" Without giving it a thought I invariably say, "I hope so." It has happened so many times I feel it truly expresses our individual ways of dealing with problems. Matthew is the thinker, Hillary the knower, Grandpa the hoper.

I told them my parable of the year 2020—with embellishments and explanations—and asked them, "Do you think people will be able to change things soon enough so the birds will be saved?"

Matthew said, "I think so." Hillary said, "I know so." I hope so!

Index.